Understanding ADA 508 website requirements and
the impact on your business

508 Remediation

A Beginner's Guide to
Understanding Web Accessibility

Jenny Hale Woldt

Testimonials

"I so much appreciate your willingness to do the remediation on our newsletter. I know the students and former students find it to be of great value!"
- T. Jack, Director of Communications, Tennessee School for the Blind

"Working with Splash Box makes the remediation process easy. I never worry about our compliance because I know I can trust their experts to get it right. Thank you for making the process so simple!"
– K. Dossett, Marketing Director, Alignment Health Plan

"Splash Box Marketing stepped in and took the weight of Section 508 compliance off our shoulders. Their attention to detail and understanding of the requirements were top-notch. They delivered high-quality work on time, every time."
– L. Pamanian, Marketing Director, Zing Health Plan

"Working with Splash Box Marketing was a game-changer. The team was knowledgeable, responsive, and genuinely cared about making our digital presence accessible to everyone. We couldn't be happier with the results."
- R. Ornelas, Sr Manager, AltaMed

Copyright Information

508 Accessibility: Understanding ADA 508 website requirements and the impact on your business by Jenny Hale Woldt

Published by Jenny Hale Woldt and Splash Box Marketing

114 Canfield Pl, Suite B9, Hendersonville, TN 37075

splashbox.com

jennyhalewoldt.com

This book was written with some assistance from AI.

Dedication

To my Splash Box Marketing family for your exceptional work, training and kindness. You are an inspiration to me. Your dedication and tenacity empower me every day to get out there and share our services with the government and private sector.

To Craig Woldt, who took a chance on me, quit his job and took on the position of CTO at Splash Box Marketing to develop our 508 Remediation program in 2012. God truly blessed me with a supportive husband and business partner. Thank you for the hours of constant research you do to keep us on top of all the regulations and changes in this field.

My special thanks to my remediation team and your commitment to making the internet accessible to the hard sight. To Helen Bowen for helping me pull this book together with your extensive knowledge of 508, you did a fantastic job. To Kenny Thomas for your continued support in developing new areas of expertise for our team and being a great team leader. To Juliana Porreca who puts on lots of different hats without complaint and has dedicated herself to taking her 508 knowledge beyond our doors and into the music space as well. To Teasha Moody who is always ready and willing to learn something new with a smile on her face and makes sure we are sending out quality work every day.

To my design team that keeps in mind the special needs of our senior focused end users and hard of sight community in every design they create. You guys are spectacular, and I love your dedication to making sure we are on brand and putting out top notch designs. My special thanks to Erica Oldham who always goes the extra mile and extra time to meet the needs of our clients and is such a blessing to the team she leads. To Karolina Kay who is my "OG" designer that I have watched grow into an amazing creative who is always willing to tackle new design technology. To Charles Cook whose patience and attention to detail makes us look great every day.

To my support team that supplies the backbone to our company and helps Splash Box present itself in a consistent voice with integrity. To Jessie Moser who helps me hold it all together and manages our wonderful clients while assisting me in keeping all the balls in the air. To Shelby Ruch who provides a professional voice for our clients with a dedication to their brands and all their many different writing style needs and is always happy to jump on niche projects with me.

Table of Contents

Testimonials 2

Copyright Information 3

Dedication 4

Table of Contents 6

My Promise To You 9

Who am I and Why Did I Write This Book? 10

What is Accessibility? 12

Principles of Web Accessibility 12

Importance of Accessible Design 13

Essential Accessibility Features 14

Challenges and Considerations 14

Conclusion 15

Digital Accessibility Laws: Section 508 and ADA Compliance ... 16

Section 508 of the Rehabilitation Act 16

Key Provisions 16

Americans with Disabilities Act (ADA) 16

Relevant Titles 17

The Intersection of Section 508 and the ADA 17

Section 508 vs. ADA: Key Differences 17

Who Must Comply with Accessibility Laws? 18

Consequences of Non-Compliance 19

Conclusion 20

Why Web Accessibility Matters for Businesses 21

Business Benefits of Accessibility 21

Financial and Competitive Advantages........................21

The Risks of Non-Compliance.......................................22

Conclusion...22

Web Content Accessibility Guidelines (WCAG) 2.0:
An Overview..23

History of WCAG 23

WCAG 2.0 Guidelines 24

Future Directions of WCAG...26

Conclusion...26

Steps for Evaluating and Assessing Accessibility.........................28

Conclusion...31

Accessibility Software & Tools 32

Automated Accessibility Testing Tools......................32

Color Contrast Analyzers..33

Screen Reader Testing 34

Keyboard Navigation Testing 35

Accessibility Evaluation Checklists 36

Conclusion...36

Enhancing Document Accessibility...................................38

Applicable WCAG Guidelines for PDFs 38

How to Tell If a Document Is Accessible....................39

Accessibility Reports — How to Run Them and Why
It Matters..44

Remediation Tools for PDF Accessibility 47

Testing Tools for PDF Accessibility...........................48

Best Practices for Creating Accessible PDFs.............49

Conclusion 49

Common Accessibility Errors.......................................51

Errors Frequently Missed by Automated Checkers...................53

Conclusion 54

Ensuring Long-Term Web Accessibility: Challenges
and Solutions 55

Challenges in Maintaining Web Accessibility 55

Best Practices for Maintaining Long-Term Accessibility........56

Benefits of Outsourcing Accessibility Remediation.................59

Selecting the Right Accessibility Remediation Partner...........59

Fostering a Culture of Accessibility Within
Your Organization 61

Conclusion 62

Appendix – HHS 508 Accessibility Checklists 63

Adobe PDF 63

Microsoft Excel..71

Microsoft PowerPoint 79

Microsoft Word...85

Web Sites, Web Applications, & Software 94

Additional Resources 105

Jenny Hale Woldt...106

Helen Bowen...107

My Promise To You

As a business owner, executive, or part of the IT team tasked with web accessibility, I know you probably already have a lot on your plate. You may be supervising employees, setting objectives for the upcoming year, managing finances, doing market research, responding to customer inquiries, and even more. You probably feel like you don't have time to learn a whole new technology or develop a new skill set and yet here you are.

It is my goal to empower you by giving you an understanding of web accessibility so you can take the next steps that make sense for your company. Whether that is hiring a company like Splash Box Marketing (shameless plug), will take care of all the accessibility issues or hiring an in-house team to do the work or as a starting point for you to take this on. With all these scenarios, you need to understand web and document accessibility so you can make the best choice and oversee whoever you decide to have do the work.

In this short book, I'll walk you through the basic principles of Web Accessibility, why it matters, and its secret benefits. I'll explain how to get started, common pitfalls you might hit and how to avoid them, and best practices in outsourcing your work to give you back your time. Finally, I'll give you tips on staying up-to-date in the ever-changing accessibility landscape and making accessibility part of your culture.

In other words, my promise to you is I'm going to tell you exactly what you need to know to get started with website accessibility and how it can serve you in a multitude of ways you may have never considered.

Who am I and Why Did I Write This Book?

In 2012, I found myself in a similar situation that you may be in right now, struggling to understand what 508 Remediation and web accessibility meant. Since 2006, I have owned the creative ad agency Splash Box Marketing. We are experts in providing beautiful graphic design pieces with quick turnaround at great prices. We were not, however, a 508 Remediation company when we started.

That all changed in 2012 when I was in a meeting with a client that had recently been fined by a governing agency for not being 508 compliant. They had no idea what 508 remediation was and, to their disappointment, neither did I. They asked me to research it, put together a plan, find resources, and develop a budget for meeting this requirement. I had my marching orders and set out to find answers.

At that point, there were no books on the market, very little information online, and few vendors to assist. Because it was such a niche industry, only a few companies offered remediation services, and they were charging exorbitant prices - upwards of $70 to $150 a page. I've seen documents needing remediation hit over 9000 pages, bringing potential quotes from $630,000 to $1,350,000.

I returned to my client armed with my findings and asked how they wanted to proceed. They came back and said, "We want YOUR company to provide this service." I was surprised, to say the least. Never one to shy away from a challenge, I accepted their request and set out to become certified in the 508 remediation software on the market at that time and learn how best to make my client compliant before their fine turned into a lawsuit.

Fast forward to today and that client continues to be 508 compliant due to our monthly work together, and at a fraction of the price than the original quotes would have us believe. Since that time my team has grown considerably and has helped 100+ business and government entities become accessible to the hard-of-sight community and make good on our slogan, "Accessibility, it's not just the law, it's the right thing to do."

I decided to write this book to be the resource I was looking for when I got into remediation, using my years of expertise and dedicated research to give you the quick, financially conscious solutions you need to feel empowered to move forward.

What is Accessibility?

Web accessibility ensures that websites and web applications are usable by all individuals, including those with disabilities. This practice enables people with diverse abilities to perceive, understand, navigate, and interact with the web effectively.

Principles of Web Accessibility

The Web Content Accessibility Guidelines (WCAG) outline four foundational principles, known by the acronym POUR, to guide accessible web design:

- **Perceivable:** Information and user interface components must be presented in ways that users can perceive, accommodating those who may rely on a single sense.

- **Operable:** Users must be able to operate interface components and navigate the site, ensuring functionality for those who may not use traditional input devices.

- **Understandable:** Content and controls should be clear and comprehensible, aiding users in processing information and interacting without confusion.

- **Robust:** Content must be robust enough to function reliably with various user agents, including assistive technologies, and adapt to evolving technologies.

Adhering to these principles helps create accessible web environments that are functional for a broad spectrum of users.

Importance of Accessible Design

Implementing accessible design is crucial for several reasons:

- **Legal and Ethical Responsibility**: Accessibility is recognized as a fundamental human right. Ensuring digital inclusivity aligns with legal standards and ethical practices, promoting equal access for all individuals.

- **Enhanced User Experience**: Accessible design often leads to improved universal usability. For instance, providing sufficient color contrast benefits users in various lighting conditions, and captions aid both individuals with hearing impairments and those in noisy environments. This is referred to in the accessibility world as the curb-cut effect, which describes how accessibility features like curb cuts, closed captioning, etc., benefit a wider demographic of people than just those with the relevant disability.

- **Expanded Audience Reach**: By removing barriers, accessible websites can tap into new markets and opportunities and reach a wider audience, including the sixteen percent of the population with disabilities.

In the context of remote work, accessible design has become even more critical. As more interactions move online, ensuring that digital platforms are accessible allows individuals with disabilities to participate fully in remote work environments. This includes access to virtual meetings, online collaboration tools, and digital resources. Organizations that prioritize accessibility in their remote work infrastructure can be proud to comply with legal standards and foster an inclusive workplace culture.

Essential Accessibility Features

Incorporating the following features can significantly improve web accessibility:

- **Text Alternatives:** Provide alternative text for non-text content, including charts, graphs, and images, to ensure that screen readers can convey the information to users with visual impairments.

- **Keyboard Accessibility:** Ensure that all functionalities are operable through a keyboard-only interface on behalf of users who cannot use a mouse.

- **Readable Content:** Use clear and straightforward language, organize content logically, and provide mechanisms for users to find content easily, such as bookmarks and logical headings.

- **Adaptable Content:** Create content that can be presented in different ways without losing information or structure, such as through assistive technologies.

- **Distinguishable Elements:** Make it easier for users to see and hear content, including visually separating foreground from background and ensuring sufficient color contrast.

Challenges and Considerations

Despite its importance, achieving web accessibility presents challenges:

- **Awareness and Education**: Designers and developers may lack knowledge about accessible design practices, unconsciously creating barriers for users with disabilities.

- **Resource Allocation**: Implementing accessibility features may require additional resources, including time and financial investment. However, the long-term benefits of inclusivity and compliance often outweigh these initial costs.

- **Keeping Pace with Technology**: As technology evolves, continuous effort is needed to ensure that new tools and platforms remain accessible to all users.

Web accessibility is a vital aspect of modern web development, ensuring that digital spaces are inclusive and usable by everyone, regardless of their abilities. By embracing accessible design principles, organizations not only fulfill legal and ethical obligations but also enhance the user experience and broaden their reach. Overcoming challenges through education, resource commitment, and adaptive strategies is essential in creating a web that truly serves all users.

Conclusion

Web accessibility is not merely an optional feature but a fundamental requirement for creating inclusive digital experiences. By adhering to the principles outlined in the Web Content Accessibility Guidelines (WCAG), organizations and developers can ensure that their websites and web applications accommodate users of all abilities. Beyond compliance with legal and ethical standards, accessible design enhances usability, expands audience reach, and fosters inclusivity in digital spaces. As remote work and online interactions continue to grow, prioritizing accessibility is essential for equitable participation in the digital landscape. Although challenges such as awareness gaps, resource constraints, and evolving technology persist, they can be addressed through proactive education, strategic investment, and ongoing adaptation. By making accessibility a core consideration in web development, we move closer to a digital world that is truly usable by everyone, regardless of their abilities.

Digital Accessibility Laws:
Section 508 and ADA Compliance

Section 508 of the Rehabilitation Act

The Rehabilitation Act was enacted in 1973 and amended in 1998 to include web accessibility. Section 508 mandates that all federal agencies develop, procure, maintain, and utilize information and communications technology (ICT) that is accessible to individuals with disabilities, regardless of whether they are federal employees or members of the public. This requirement ensures that everyone has comparable access to information and services.

Key Provisions

- **Scope**: Section 508 applies to all federal agencies and encompasses a wide range of ICT, including websites, software applications, multimedia, and electronic documents.

- **Standards Alignment**: The Section 508 Standards are harmonized with the Web Content Accessibility Guidelines (WCAG) 2.0, Level AA, ensuring consistency in accessibility criteria.

- **Compliance Obligations**: Federal agencies must regularly assess and report on their ICT accessibility, integrating accessibility considerations into their procurement processes and development lifecycles.

Americans with Disabilities Act (ADA)

The ADA, enacted in 1990, is a comprehensive civil rights law prohibiting discrimination based on disability across various sectors, including employment, public services, and public accommodations. While the ADA does not explicitly mention digital accessibility, its provisions have been interpreted to encompass websites and online services, especially under Titles II and III.

Relevant Titles

- **Title II**: Pertains to state and local governments, mandating that their services, programs, and activities be accessible to individuals with disabilities. This has been extended to include accessible digital services and online content.

- **Title III**: Addresses public entities operated by private bodies, such as businesses and nonprofits, requiring that their facilities (and by extension, their websites and digital offerings) be accessible to people with disabilities.

The Intersection of Section 508 and the ADA

While both laws aim to prevent discrimination, Section 508 specifically targets federal agencies and provides detailed technical standards for compliance. In contrast, the ADA applies to a broader scope of various public and private entities, with its digital accessibility requirements evolving through legal interpretations and enforcement actions. Entities covered by both laws must ensure their digital content meets the applicable accessibility standards to provide equal access to individuals with disabilities.

Section 508 vs. ADA: Key Differences

Aspect	Section 508	ADA
Applies To	Federal agencies & contractors	Public & private entities
Scope	ICT, including software & websites	Broader anti-discrimination law
Legal Basis	Specific compliance standards (WCAG)	Interpreted case by case

Who Must Comply with Accessibility Laws?

Ensuring digital accessibility is essential for various entities, including:

1. Federal Agencies and Contractors

- **Obligations:** All federal agencies must ensure their electronic and information technology is accessible, including websites, applications, and multimedia.

- **Contractor Requirements:** Private companies providing digital services to federal agencies must also meet Section 508 standards.

2. State and Local Governments Receiving Federal Funding

Government entities receiving federal funding must comply with both Title II of the ADA and Section 508, ensuring accessible online public services.

3. Educational Institutions

- **Higher Education:** Colleges and universities receiving federal aid must ensure equitable access to learning management systems, digital coursework, and communication tools for all students.

- **K-12 Schools:** Public schools receiving federal funds must provide accessible digital resources for students with disabilities.

4. Private Businesses and ADA Compliance

Retailers, restaurants, healthcare providers, and other businesses must maintain accessible websites, as courts have ruled that inaccessible websites violate the ADA.

Consequences of Non-Compliance

In 2024, over a thousand web accessibility lawsuits were filed. While this is a decrease from 2023, which saw over two thousand cases, almost 48% of filings were against companies who had previously been sued for accessibility issues, indicating companies' struggles with long-term compliance. The most impacted industry was consumer durables & apparel, followed closely by food, beverage, & tobacco and retail. Notably, these are all non-government entities, demonstrating the wide reach of ADA and Section 508 legislation.

A notable example underscoring the legal and financial risks of ADA noncompliance is the 2017 lawsuit *Access Now, Inc. v. Blue Apron, LLC*. This case became a pivotal moment in web accessibility litigation because Blue Apron operated solely online, without any physical storefront. The company argued that, in the absence of a brick-and-mortar location, its website should not be subject to Title III of the Americans with Disabilities Act, which governs access to public accommodations. However, the court rejected this argument and denied the motion to dismiss, reinforcing the precedent that digital spaces can be held to the same accessibility standards as physical ones.

This ruling sent a clear message: businesses cannot overlook the accessibility of their online platforms. Failure to comply with ADA requirements—regardless of whether operations are conducted in physical or digital spaces—can result in significant legal consequences and reputational damage.

By understanding who must comply with Section 508 and related ADA regulations, organizations can proactively address digital accessibility, ensuring equal access for all users and mitigating legal risks.

Conclusion

Section 508 of the Rehabilitation Act and the Americans with Disabilities Act (ADA) serve as critical frameworks for ensuring digital accessibility and preventing discrimination against individuals with disabilities. While Section 508 establishes explicit technical standards for federal agencies and contractors, the ADA extends accessibility requirements to a broader range of public and private entities, reinforcing the importance of equitable digital access.

With an increasing reliance on digital platforms for government services, education, and commerce, compliance with these laws is both a legal obligation and a strategic necessity. Organizations that fail to meet accessibility standards not only risk legal consequences, including lawsuits and enforcement actions, but also exclude a significant portion of the population from essential services.

Despite challenges such as ongoing legal interpretations, evolving technology, and reliance on insufficient accessibility overlays, entities covered under Section 508 and the ADA can achieve compliance through proactive measures. Implementing accessible web design, integrating WCAG guidelines, and continuously evaluating digital accessibility ensures an inclusive user experience for all individuals, regardless of ability. By prioritizing accessibility, organizations can foster inclusivity, expand their reach, and uphold their legal and ethical responsibilities in the digital age.

Why Web Accessibility Matters for Businesses

In the digital age, web accessibility has become a critical consideration for businesses aiming to reach a broad audience and maintain a positive reputation. Ensuring that websites are accessible to all users, including those with disabilities, not only fulfills ethical and legal obligations but also offers substantial business advantages. Conversely, neglecting accessibility can lead to significant risks, including legal challenges and financial losses.

Business Benefits of Accessibility

- **Market Expansion:** Over 28% of U.S. adults have a disability. By committing to web accessibility, you open your business to a much wider customer base.

- **Improved Brand Reputation:** In 2018, the Edelman communications firm found that 64 percent of consumers are willing to support or boycott a brand based on their sociopolitical stances, indicating just how important it is to publicly stand for the right thing.

Financial and Competitive Advantages

- **Increased Revenue**: Accessible websites attract more customers, leading to higher sales. Additionally, people grow more likely to develop disabilities with age, and ensuring your website is accessible allows you to retain those long-term customers as they evolve.

- **Better User Experience**: Clear navigation and alt text benefit all users, not just those with disabilities. Over 50% of online shoppers are mobile users, and the web accessibility focus on mobile navigation creates a more fluid user experience for those valuable customers.

The Risks of Non-Compliance

- **Legal and Financial Penalties**: Companies that fail to provide accessible digital services may face lawsuits and hefty fines.

- **Reputation Damage**: A lawsuit or complaint negatively impacts brand perception and customer trust.

By prioritizing web accessibility, businesses not only fulfill their legal obligations but also enhance their market reach, improve user experience, and protect their brand reputation. The proactive adoption of accessible design is a strategic investment that yields significant returns in today's inclusive digital landscape.

Conclusion

Web accessibility is no longer just a compliance requirement; it is a strategic business necessity. By ensuring that digital platforms are accessible to all users, including the 26% of U.S. adults with disabilities, businesses can expand their customer base, enhance user experience, and strengthen brand reputation.

Beyond legal obligations, accessibility fosters inclusivity, builds customer loyalty, and creates a competitive advantage in the marketplace. Companies prioritizing accessibility benefit from increased revenue opportunities and a broader audience reach, while those that neglect it face potential lawsuits, financial penalties, and reputational harm.

Investing in accessible design is not just about meeting regulations; it is about future-proofing businesses for a more inclusive digital world. By proactively addressing accessibility, organizations can drive long-term success while ensuring equal access for all.

Web Content Accessibility Guidelines (WCAG) 2.0: An Overview

History of WCAG

- **1999: WCAG 1.0:** The W3C introduced WCAG 1.0 in May 1999, establishing the first set of guidelines aimed at enhancing web accessibility. This initial version focused on HTML-based content and provided 14 guidelines to assist developers in creating accessible web content.

- **2008: WCAG 2.0:** Recognizing the rapid evolution of web technologies, the W3C released WCAG 2.0 in December 2008. This version expanded its scope beyond HTML, adopting a technology-agnostic approach to address various web content types. WCAG 2.0 introduced four foundational principles (Perceivable, Operable, Understandable, and Robust (POUR)) to guide accessible web design.

- **2018: WCAG 2.1:** To address emerging accessibility challenges, WCAG 2.1 was published in June 2018. This update built upon WCAG 2.0, introducing additional success criteria to improve accessibility for users with cognitive and learning disabilities, low vision, and those accessing content on mobile devices.

- **2023: WCAG 2.2:** WCAG 2.2 was released in October 2023, including new criteria for conformance and changes to conformance level minimums. Changes were made in the areas of keyboard focus, input modalities, predictability, and input assistance to better address the needs of those using keyboard navigation and other non-mouse input options.

WCAG 2.0 Guidelines

WCAG 2.0 is structured around four core principles, each encompassing specific guidelines and success criteria designed to ensure web content is accessible to a diverse user base.

1. Perceivable

Objective: Present information and user interface components in ways that users can perceive.

Examples:

- Adaptable Content: Ensure content can be presented in different ways without losing meaning, allowing users to customize their experience according to their needs.

- Distinguishable Elements: Make it easier for users to see and hear content by separating foreground from background, enhancing readability and comprehension.

- Text Alternatives: Provide text alternatives for non-text content, enabling assistive technologies to convey information effectively.

- Time-Based Media: Offer alternatives for time-based media, such as captions for videos and transcripts for audio content, to accommodate users with hearing impairments.

2. Operable

Objective: Ensure user interface components and navigation are operable.

Examples:

- Enough Time: Provide users with sufficient time to read and use content, accommodating those with slower reading speeds or cognitive challenges.

- Keyboard Accessibility: Make all functionality available from a keyboard, assisting users who cannot use a mouse.

- Navigable Content: Help users navigate, find content, and determine their location within a website, enhancing the overall user experience.

- Seizure Prevention: Avoid designing content that could cause seizures, such as flashing visuals, to protect users with photosensitive epilepsy.

3. Understandable

Objective: Make information and the operation of the user interface understandable.

Examples:

- Input Assistance: Assist users in avoiding and correcting mistakes, particularly in forms and data entry fields, to enhance accuracy and reduce frustration.

- Predictable Web Pages: Create web pages that appear and operate in predictable ways, reducing cognitive load and confusion.

- Readable Text: Ensure text is readable and understandable, using clear and concise language.

4. Robust

Objective: Develop content to be robust enough to be interpreted reliably by a wide variety of user agents, including assistive technologies.

Examples:

- Browser and Technology Compatibility: Ensure that your content functions on all web browsers, including outmoded and rarer options, and assistive technologies.

- Coding: Confirm that your website's code is semantically well-written, using complete tags and the correct nesting structure.

Each principle encompasses specific guidelines and success criteria, which are categorized into three conformance levels:

- **Level A**: Addresses the most basic web accessibility features.

- **Level AA**: Deals with the biggest and most common barriers for disabled users. This is the standard under Section 508.

- **Level AAA**: Tackles the highest and most complex level of web accessibility.

Future Directions of WCAG

The dynamic nature of technology and user needs necessitates the continuous evolution of accessibility guidelines. The W3C is actively working on WCAG 3.0, aiming to provide a more flexible and comprehensive framework that addresses a broader spectrum of disabilities and adapts to emerging technologies. Future guidelines are expected to place greater emphasis on mobile device accessibility, reflecting the increasing reliance on smartphones and tablets for web access. As technologies such as virtual reality and artificial intelligence become more prevalent, their accessibility is also expected to be a focal point in upcoming guidelines.

By adhering to WCAG 2.0 and its updates, organizations can create accessible, user-friendly web content, fostering a more inclusive digital environment for all users.

Conclusion

The evolution of the Web Content Accessibility Guidelines (WCAG) reflects the ongoing commitment to making digital content accessible to all users, including those with disabilities.

Since the introduction of WCAG 1.0 in 1999, the guidelines have continuously adapted to the changing technological landscape, ensuring that accessibility standards remain relevant and effective. Each iteration, from WCAG 2.0 to the latest WCAG 2.2, has introduced enhancements that address emerging challenges, from mobile accessibility to improved support for users relying on assistive technologies.

By following the core principles of perceivability, operability, understandability, and robustness (POUR), organizations can create digital experiences that are both inclusive and user-friendly. Conformance levels provide a structured approach to accessibility, guiding developers and content creators in implementing the most critical accessibility features.

Looking ahead, the development of WCAG 3.0 signals the continued evolution of accessibility standards, ensuring that digital environments accommodate the growing diversity of users and technologies. As accessibility becomes an increasingly integral aspect of web design and development, adherence to WCAG principles will not only fulfill legal and ethical responsibilities but also contribute to a more inclusive and equitable digital world.

Steps for Evaluating and Assessing Accessibility

Ensuring web accessibility requires a structured and methodical approach. By following a step-by-step process, organizations can identify, prioritize, and resolve accessibility barriers effectively, making their digital content inclusive for all users.

1. Define the Evaluation Scope

Before assessing accessibility, determine the scope of the evaluation. Consider:

- **High-Traffic Pages**: Pages with the most user engagement.

- **Critical User Task Pages**: Essential areas such as checkout pages, login portals, and contact forms.

- **Reported Issues**: Pages that have received accessibility complaints from users.

- **Downloadable Documents**: Determine how many PDFs, Word, Excel, and PowerPoint documents are attached to the website and need to be remediated.

2. Explore the Website

Understanding the website's structure, functionality, and user demographics is crucial. This step helps in:

- Identifying key accessibility barriers.

- Recognizing the needs of different user groups.

- Prioritizing critical accessibility improvements.

3. Select a Representative Sample

Since auditing an entire website may not always be feasible, choose a set of diverse pages that reflect the site's content and functionality. A representative sample should include:

- The homepage.

- Key navigation elements.

- Forms and interactive features.

- Multimedia content such as videos and images.

4. Conduct an Accessibility Audit

Evaluate the selected sample against the Web Content Accessibility Guidelines (WCAG) using multiple testing methods:

- **Automated Testing**: Use accessibility evaluation tools to identify obvious issues such as missing alt text, color contrast problems, and keyboard navigation barriers.

- **Manual Testing**: Conduct expert reviews to assess aspects that automated tools might miss, such as the accuracy of alternative text and the logical structure of headings.

- **User Testing**: Engage individuals with disabilities to test the website and provide direct feedback on real-world usability challenges.

5. Prioritize Issues

Not all accessibility issues have the same impact. Prioritize fixes based on:

- **High-Impact Barriers**: Issues that prevent users from completing essential tasks (e.g., inaccessible login forms).

- **Quick Wins**: Simple, high-value improvements that can be implemented with minimal effort (e.g., adding missing alt text, adjusting color contrast issues, removing flashing graphics).

- **Legal Compliance Requirements**: Fixes necessary to align with accessibility laws and regulations such as WCAG 2.1 AA, ADA, and Section 508.

6. Develop a Remediation Plan

Once issues are identified and prioritized, outline a structured remediation plan, including:

- **Actionable Steps**: Determine clear tasks for resolving each issue.

- **Resource Allocation**: Assign responsibilities to developers, content creators, and designers OR find and hire a professional 508 remediation company.

- **Timeline and Milestones**: Set deadlines to track progress and ensure timely completion.

7. Implement Changes

After planning, execute the necessary changes to the website's design, content, and code. Before deployment:

- Test all updates using automated and manual methods.

- Ensure compliance with accessibility standards.

- Conduct another round of user testing for validation.

8. Continuous Monitoring and Maintenance

Web accessibility is an ongoing effort, not a one-time fix. Maintain accessibility by:

- Regularly testing pages for compliance with evolving WCAG standards.

- Gathering user feedback to address new challenges.

- Keeping up with technological advancements that may impact accessibility.

Conclusion

Improving web accessibility is a continuous process that requires thoughtful evaluation, strategic prioritization, and proactive remediation. By systematically defining the evaluation scope, conducting thorough audits, prioritizing issues, and implementing structured improvements, organizations can create an inclusive digital experience for all users. With ongoing monitoring and adaptation, accessibility remains a core element of user-centered design, fostering greater inclusivity and compliance with evolving standards.

Accessibility Software & Tools

Automated accessibility testing tools play a crucial role in identifying and addressing web accessibility barriers. These tools provide a fast and efficient way to detect common issues, ensuring that websites meet accessibility standards and provide an inclusive experience for all users. While automated testing can highlight structural problems, it should be complemented with manual evaluations and user testing to achieve a comprehensive assessment.

Automated Accessibility Testing Tools

Automated testing tools provide a fast and efficient way to detect common accessibility issues across websites. While they can identify structural problems, they should be supplemented with manual testing for a complete evaluation.

- **WAVE (Web Accessibility Evaluation Tool):** WAVE is a browser-based tool that highlights accessibility issues by overlaying icons and annotations directly onto a web page. It detects problems such as missing alternative text for images, incorrect heading structures, and low contrast ratios. WAVE also provides detailed explanations of each issue, helping web developers and content creators understand and resolve accessibility barriers.

- **Axe by Deque:** Axe is an accessibility testing engine widely used by developers. It integrates with web browsers and development environments to scan pages for WCAG violations. Axe provides actionable recommendations for resolving errors, making it a valuable tool for organizations working toward compliance with accessibility standards.

Actionable Insights:

- **Integrate Testing into Development:** Incorporate automated testing tools into your development workflow to identify and address accessibility issues early.

- **Regular Audits.** Perform regular accessibility audits using these tools to maintain compliance as content and features evolve.

Color Contrast Analyzers

Proper color contrast ensures that text and visual elements remain legible for users with visual impairments, including color blindness. Color contrast analyzers help designers and developers evaluate whether color combinations meet accessibility guidelines.

- **A11Y Color Contrast Validator:** This tool assesses the contrast between text and background colors to determine if they meet WCAG guidelines. It is useful for ensuring that websites, digital documents, and user interfaces remain readable for users with low vision.

- **Contrast Checker:** A simple tool that allows users to enter foreground and background colors to calculate contrast ratios. This tool helps designers select accessible color schemes that enhance readability and usability.

Actionable Insights:

- **Design with Accessibility in Mind:** Use color contrast analyzers during the design phase to select accessible color palettes.

- **Test All Text Elements:** Ensure that all textual content meets the recommended contrast ratios, including text over images or gradients.

Screen Reader Testing

Approximately 8% of the United States population experiences some form of visual impairment, making it essential to consider their needs in digital content. One widely used accessibility tool is the screen reader, which reads on-screen content aloud or connects to a refreshable braille display for users who are both visually and hearing impaired. Screen readers typically begin reading from the top of a webpage and proceed downward; however, users can navigate more efficiently by using keyboard shortcuts to jump to specific elements such as headers, links, tables, and figures.

This highlights the critical importance of proper tagging order. A common misconception is that screen readers follow the reading order defined by software such as Adobe Acrobat, when in fact, they rely solely on the document's tag tree. Ensuring content is tested with screen readers helps verify that pages are properly structured and that non-text elements include meaningful, descriptive tags.

- **NVDA (NonVisual Desktop Access):** NVDA is a free, open-source screen reader for Windows. It enables developers and accessibility specialists to test how their web content is experienced by users who rely on assistive technology. NVDA reads text, identifies interactive elements, and verifies whether websites offer a logical and intuitive experience.

- **JAWS (Job Access With Speech):** JAWS is a widely used screen reader designed for Windows. It offers advanced features for browsing websites, reading documents, and interacting with digital interfaces. Testing with JAWS ensures that websites accommodate users with visual impairments by providing proper labeling and navigation support.

- **VoiceOver:** VoiceOver is a native screen reader in the Mac OS operating system and is navigable via keyboard commands. It can be used to read and edit text, find item descriptions, and select buttons. It is also compatible with select refreshable braille displays using contracted or uncontracted braille.

Actionable Insights:

- **Conduct Regular Screen Reader Testing:** Regularly test web content with screen readers to ensure compatibility and usability.

- **Provide Descriptive Text Equivalents:** Ensure that all non-text content, such as images and multimedia, have descriptive alt text or transcripts.

Keyboard Navigation Testing

Many users, including individuals with motor disabilities, rely on keyboard navigation instead of a mouse. Testing for keyboard accessibility ensures that all interactive elements, such as links, buttons, and form fields, are fully operable using only keyboard commands.

- **Manual Keyboard Testing:** This involves navigating a website using the "Tab" key to ensure that all interactive elements are reachable in a logical sequence. Proper focus indicators should be visible, and no element should trap the user, preventing them from navigating away.

- **Keyboard Testing Extensions:** Some browser-based tools analyze keyboard navigation by highlighting focus order and identifying elements that are not accessible via the keyboard. These tools provide insights into improving navigation for users who rely on keyboard input.

Actionable Insights:

- **Test All Interactive Elements:** Ensure that all interactive components, such as links, buttons, and form fields, are accessible via keyboard.

- **Logical Focus Order:** Verify that the navigation order is logical and intuitive, following the visual layout of the page.

- **Visible Focus Indicators:** Ensure that focus indicators are visible, helping users track their position on the page during navigation.

Accessibility Evaluation Checklists

Checklists offer a structured approach to ensuring compliance with accessibility guidelines. They serve as a reference for designers, developers, and content creators to systematically review web content. The WCAG Compliance Checklist outlines WCAG success criteria across compliance levels (A, AA, AAA). It helps teams track their progress in meeting accessibility standards and ensures that all critical barriers are addressed. The United States Health and Human Services has published such checklists, which can be found in the appendix.

By using these tools, professionals can effectively evaluate and enhance web accessibility, creating a more inclusive digital experience for all users. Implementing accessibility improvements benefits not only individuals with disabilities but also enhances usability for a broader audience.

Conclusion

Accessibility testing tools are essential for creating an inclusive digital experience, helping organizations identify and address accessibility barriers efficiently. While automated tools like WAVE and Axe provide valuable insights, they should be supplemented with manual testing and user feedback to capture more nuanced issues. Regular audits, structured evaluation checklists, and a comprehensive testing strategy ensure compliance with accessibility standards while enhancing usability for a wider audience. By prioritizing accessibility testing, businesses not only meet legal requirements but also foster digital inclusivity, improve user experience, and ensure equal access for all users.

Enhancing Document Accessibility

An interesting component of web accessibility is PDF, Word, Excel, and PowerPoint documents that are attached as downloadable files to a website. Even if your entire website is coded and designed for accessibility, if a user clicks into a document and is unable to read and navigate it, that creates an accessibility problem. Ensuring that these documents are accessible is crucial for inclusivity, allowing individuals with disabilities to access and interact with content effectively and in a similar manner to a sighted person.

Applicable WCAG Guidelines for PDFs

The WCAG provides a comprehensive framework to make web content more accessible. Key guidelines pertinent to PDF documents include:

- **Perceivable:** Ensure that information and user interface components are presented in ways that users can perceive.

  - **Text Alternatives:** Provide text alternatives for non-text content, such as images, to allow screen readers to convey information effectively.

  - **Adaptable:** Create content that can be presented in different ways without losing information or structure, ensuring compatibility with various assistive technologies.

- **Operable:** Make all functionalities available from a keyboard, ensuring that users who cannot use a mouse can navigate and interact with the document.

  - **Keyboard Accessible:** Ensure that all interactive elements, such as links and form fields, are operable through keyboard navigation.

- **Understandable**: Make text content readable and understandable.

  - **Readable:** Use clear and simple language and provide definitions for unusual terms or abbreviations to aid comprehension.

- **Robust**: Content must be robust enough to be interpreted reliably by a wide variety of user agents, including assistive technologies.

  - **Compatible:** Ensure documents are compatible with current and future user tools, adhering to established accessibility standards.

How to Tell If a Document Is Accessible

Creating accessible documents is essential for ensuring that everyone, including people with disabilities, can access and understand content. But how can you tell if a document is truly accessible? This chapter outlines a practical, step-by-step approach to identifying the key markers of accessibility in digital documents—especially PDFs and Word files—using built-in tools and visual inspections.

Step 1: Check for Bookmark Navigation

Why it matters: Bookmarks help users, especially those using screen readers, navigate long documents more efficiently.

What to do:

- Open the document in your PDF viewer (e.g., Adobe Acrobat).

- Look for a panel or tab labeled Bookmarks or Navigation Pane – it should have opened automatically.

- If bookmarks are present, verify that they match the document's structure (e.g., headings, sections).

Step 2: Try to Select the Text

Why it matters: If you can't select text, the content may be embedded as an image, making it inaccessible to screen readers and search functions.

What to do:

- Use your mouse to click and drag over text in the document.

- If the text cannot be highlighted, it is likely a scanned image or flattened layer.

Step 3: Hover Over Images to Check for Alt Text

Why it matters: Alternative (alt) text provides descriptive information about images for users who rely on screen readers.

What to do:

- Move your mouse pointer over an image.

- Check if a tooltip appears with a brief description of the image.

Important Notes:

- Not all viewers show alt text on hover. Use a tool like Adobe Acrobat's "Set Alternate Text" or screen reader simulation mode for a more reliable check.

- Ensure that:

  - Decorative images are marked as such.

  - Informative images have concise and meaningful descriptions.

Step 4: Review Document Metadata

Why it matters: Metadata provides important context about a document's content, language, and authorship.

What to do:

- In Adobe Acrobat, go to **File** > **Properties**.

- In the first tab, **Description**, check the following fields:

  o Title

  o Author

  o Subject

  o Keywords

- Next, click to the **Initial View** tab and check the following fields:

  o Navigation tab – should be set to "Bookmarks Panel and Page"

  o Under Window Options, "Show" should be set to "Document Title"

- Finally, click to the **Advanced** tab and check the following fields:

  o Print Page Range – should have the full page range listed

  o Language – should be set to the correct language to improve screen reader interpretation and pronunciation

Step 5: Inspect the Tag Tree

Why it matters: Tags are the backbone of accessibility in PDFs. They provide a structural representation of the document for assistive technologies.

What to do:

- Open the **Tags Panel** in Adobe Acrobat or a similar viewer.

- Look for a structured tree of tags that matches the logical reading order of the document.

  - The entire tag tree should be contained within the <Document> tag

  - Beyond that, there should be no container tags – no <Sect>, <Div>, or <Part> tags

  - The title of the document should be inside a <H1> tag

  - All other headers should be within <H2>, <H3>, etc. tags

  - All regular text should be within <P> tags

Step 6: Walk Through the Tags for Logical Order

Why it matters: Even if tags are present, they must follow a logical reading sequence for assistive technologies to interpret content correctly. It's a common misconception that screen readers use Adobe's reading order – they exclusively use the tag tree.

What to do:

- Expand the tag tree and manually navigate through each tag.

- Check if:

  - Headings are nested properly.

  - Paragraphs appear in the expected sequence.

  - Lists, tables, and other elements are tagged appropriately.

Step 7: Use Built-In Accessibility Validators

Why it matters: Automated validators catch many common issues quickly and are a good first-pass diagnostic tool.

Recommended Tools:

- Adobe Acrobat's Accessibility Checker

- Microsoft Word Accessibility Checker (under Review > Check Accessibility)

- CommonLook PDF Validator (for more advanced PDF testing)

What to do:

- Run the checker and review the results.

- Prioritize fixing:

    o Missing alt text

    o Unlabeled form fields

    o Incorrect heading structure

    o Missing document title or language

Actionable Tip: Always manually review your document even after running a checker—automation doesn't catch everything.

No single method guarantees complete accessibility, but by combining visual inspection with tool-based validation, you can significantly improve the usability and compliance of your documents. Incorporate these checks into your document creation workflow to ensure accessibility is built-in from the start—not added as an afterthought.

Accessibility Reports — How to Run Them and Why It Matters

Ensuring that digital documents are accessible is a foundational step toward inclusivity and compliance with accessibility standards. Accessibility reports offer a streamlined method for identifying and correcting accessibility barriers within PDF documents.

Why Accessibility Reports Matter

Accessibility reports serve multiple critical purposes:

- **Validation and Documentation**: A completed report can serve as documentation that accessibility checks were conducted, which is especially important in regulated environments.

- **Error Identification**: These reports highlight areas where the document may fail accessibility standards, such as missing tags or improper heading structure.

- **Improvement Roadmap**: They offer practical guidance for remediation, including links to documentation and, in some cases, automatic fixes.

- **Support Manual Checks**: While automated tools are helpful, some accessibility issues require human judgment. Reports highlight these areas for manual review.

Remember: A report alone does **not** guarantee full accessibility. It is a tool in a larger process that includes both automation and manual review.

Step-by-Step: Running an Accessibility Report in Adobe Acrobat Reader

Follow these steps to generate and interpret an accessibility report using Adobe Acrobat Reader:

1. Open the Document

- Launch Adobe Acrobat Reader.

- Open the PDF file you want to assess.

2. Access the Accessibility Tool

If "Accessibility" appears in the Tools Panel:

- Click the **Accessibility** button on the right-hand tools panel.

If "Accessibility" is not visible:

- Click **More Tools** at the bottom right of the tools panel.

- Scroll down to Protect & Standardize.

- Find **Accessibility** and click **Open**.

3. Initiate the Accessibility Check

- Click **Accessibility Check** in the new Tools Panel on the right to launch the checker dialogue.

4. Configure the Report Settings

In the Accessibility Checker dialogue window:

- Ensure the **"Create accessibility report"** checkbox is selected.

- Choose the folder where the report should be saved.

- Under Page Range, confirm All pages in document is selected.

- Check that Checking Options show 32 of 32 in all categories

5. Run the Check

- Click **Start Checking** to initiate the scan.

- The **Accessibility Checker panel** will open on the left side of the screen, displaying identified issues by category and page location.

Interpreting and Addressing Issues

Each issue identified in the report, which will appear on the left panel, comes with a menu of options. Right-click on any issue to access the following tools:

- **Pass**: Select if manual inspection confirms the element meets accessibility standards.

- **Fail**: Select if manual inspection confirms the element does *not* meet standards.

- **Fix**: Opens a dialogue (when available) to help you fix the issue; otherwise, you will see a pop-up letting you know there is not an automatic fix available.

- **Skip Rule**: Use cautiously, as this option is rarely appropriate.

- **Explain**: Opens Adobe's official documentation for the issue, offering context and resolution strategies.

- **Check Again**: Re-runs the check for that specific item after a fix has been applied.

- **Show Report**: Opens a full summary and detailed report of the current scan.

- **Options**: Reopens the checker dialogue to modify settings.

Pro Tip: Manual verification is essential. For example, while the tool can confirm that tags are present, it cannot determine whether they are in the correct logical order or properly structured for screen readers.

Final Steps

1. Make Necessary Fixes

- Address each issue using the tools provided or manually within the document.

2. Re-run the Accessibility Check

- After corrections, click **Check Again** or re-launch the checker from the Accessibility panel.

- Repeat until all critical issues are resolved.

Summary: Best Practices for Accessibility Reporting

- **Run early, run often**: Don't wait until the document is complete. Checking as you go helps avoid large-scale revisions.

- **Combine tools and judgment**: Automated tools catch many, but not all, issues. Always review flagged content manually when prompted.

- **Document your process**: Save your final accessibility report. It can serve as evidence of your compliance efforts.

By integrating accessibility checks into your regular workflow, you not only support compliance and inclusivity but also enhance the overall quality and usability of your documents.

Remediation Tools for PDF Accessibility

Achieving PDF accessibility often requires the use of specialized tools to identify and rectify issues. Notable remediation tools include:

- **AccessAltText.com**: A tool used to create dynamic alternative text for all the photos embedded within a PDF document. Using the context of the words within a document, Access Alt Text creates grammatically correct alternative text to describe the photos within a PDF document. It provides you with a Word document, so these can be copied and pasted into the appropriate locations within your document. This process saves hours of work.

- **Adobe Acrobat Pro DC**: A widely used tool that offers comprehensive features for creating and editing PDFs. It includes an accessibility checker that identifies issues and provides guidance on remediation. Users can add tags, set reading orders, and ensure that interactive elements are accessible.

- **CommonLook PDF**: A software program assisting in verifying PDF documents against accessibility standards such as WCAG and Section 508. It provides detailed reports and guides users through the remediation process to ensure compliance.

- **Equidox**: A web-based application designed to convert PDFs into accessible formats. It automates many aspects of the remediation process, including tagging and setting reading orders, making it user-friendly for those without extensive technical expertise.

Testing Tools for PDF Accessibility

After remediation, it's essential to test PDFs to confirm their accessibility. Effective testing tools include:

- **PAC 3 (PDF Accessibility Checker)**: A free tool that evaluates PDF files against PDF/UA and WCAG standards. It provides a summary of accessibility issues and offers suggestions for improvements.

- **JAWS (Job Access With Speech)**: A screen reader that allows testers to experience PDFs from the perspective of users with visual impairments, ensuring that content is navigable and comprehensible.

- **NVDA (NonVisual Desktop Access)**: Another screen reader that is free and open-source, enabling comprehensive testing of PDF accessibility features.

Best Practices for Creating Accessible PDFs

Proactive measures during the document creation process can significantly enhance PDF accessibility:

- **Use Proper Document Structure**: Apply headings, lists, and other structural elements appropriately to facilitate navigation and comprehension.

- **Provide Descriptive Alt Text**: For all non-text elements, include concise and informative alternative text to convey the purpose and content to users relying on screen readers.

- **Ensure Logical Reading Order**: Verify that the content flows in a logical sequence, especially in complex layouts, to aid users who depend on assistive technologies.

- **Embed Fonts**: Incorporate fonts within the PDF to maintain text clarity and ensure compatibility across different devices and readers.

- **Include Metadata**: Add relevant information such as the document title, author, and language settings to enhance accessibility and searchability.

Conclusion

Ensuring PDF accessibility is a multifaceted process that involves understanding applicable guidelines, utilizing appropriate remediation and testing tools, and adhering to best practices during document creation. By implementing these strategies, organizations can create inclusive content that is accessible to all users, regardless of their abilities.

Common Accessibility Errors

Ensuring digital accessibility is essential for compliance, inclusivity, and user experience. While some organizations attempt to address accessibility internally, the process is complex and fraught with potential pitfalls. Many businesses lack the expertise to implement accessibility correctly, often leading to errors that negatively impact users with disabilities. This section explores the risks associated with handling accessibility without professional assistance, including common accessibility mistakes, limitations of automated checkers, and the challenge of maintaining compliance in an evolving digital landscape.

When organizations attempt to implement accessibility without professional expertise, they often introduce errors that hinder usability. Here are some of the most common mistakes:

1. Lack of Alternative Text (Alt Text)

Alt text provides descriptions of images for screen readers, allowing visually impaired users to understand visual content. Common mistakes include:

- **Missing Alt Text**: No description is provided for images.

- **Vague Descriptions**: Descriptions like "image123.jpg" that don't convey useful information.

- **Overly Detailed Descriptions**: Providing unnecessary or irrelevant details that overwhelm users.

2. Poor Color Contrast

Low contrast between text and background can make content unreadable for users with visual impairments. Common issues include:

- **Failing to Meet Contrast Ratio**: Not meeting the minimum 4.5:1 ratio for normal text.

- Using Color as the Sole Means of Conveying Information: Relying solely on color to communicate content.

- **Neglecting to Test Contrast on Different Devices**: Not checking contrast across various screen types and settings.

3. Inaccessible Forms

Forms are critical for user interaction, but accessibility barriers often arise. Common mistakes include:

- **Lack of Properly Labeled Fields**: Fields are not clearly marked with descriptions.

- **Missing Instructions for Required Fields**: Users are unaware of what information is mandatory.

- **Failure to Ensure Keyboard Navigability**: Forms are not operable via keyboard navigation.

4. Non-Descriptive Link Text

Screen readers rely on link text to inform users about the destination. Problems occur in:

- **Vague Text**: Links use phrases like "Click here" or "Read more" without context.

- **Multiple Identical Links**: Multiple links with the same text, confusing users about their destination.

- **Lack of Focus States**: Links do not display focus states for keyboard navigation.

5. Improper Use of Headings and Structure

Headings help users navigate content efficiently. Common errors include:

- **Skipping Heading Levels**: Jumping from H1 to H3 without appropriate subheadings.

- **Using Headings for Styling**: Applying heading styles for visual purposes rather than for structure.

- **Failing to Maintain Logical Hierarchy**: Disorganized content that hinders navigation.

6. Inaccessible PDFs and Documents

PDFs often present accessibility barriers. Common issues include:

- **Lack of Proper Document Tagging**: PDFs lack structure for screen readers.

- **Missing Alt Text for Images**: Images within PDFs do not have descriptive alt text.

- **Poor Text Formatting**: Text in PDFs is not properly formatted for resizing or reflowing.

Errors Frequently Missed by Automated Checkers

Automated accessibility testing tools provide a useful first step in identifying issues, but they are not foolproof. Many errors require human judgment and manual review. Some of the most frequently missed issues include:

1. Inaccurate Alt Text
Automated checkers can detect the presence or lack thereof of alt text but cannot assess its accuracy or usefulness. Poorly written descriptions may technically pass a test but still be unhelpful for users.

2. Keyboard Navigation Issues
Many tools identify whether interactive elements are keyboard-focusable but do not test for usability. For instance, a site may allow keyboard navigation but still present a confusing or inefficient tab order.

3. **Dynamic Content and ARIA Implementation**
   Automated tools often struggle with detecting accessibility
   issues related to dynamic content, such as pop-ups and
   interactive widgets. Improper ARIA (Accessible Rich Internet
   Applications) roles and attributes can create significant
   barriers for assistive technology users.

4. **Caption and Transcript Quality**
   Tools can verify the presence of captions on videos but cannot
   assess their accuracy or synchronization. Poorly transcribed
   captions can make content unusable for deaf and hard-of-
   hearing users.

5. **Contextual Issues in Content**
   Even if all technical requirements are met, automated tools do
   not evaluate readability or clarity. A site may be technically
   accessible but still difficult to navigate due to poor design
   choices.

Conclusion

In conclusion, while digital accessibility is crucial for
compliance and inclusivity, attempting to implement it without
professional expertise can lead to significant errors that hinder
usability for individuals with disabilities. Common mistakes such
as missing alt text, poor color contrast, inaccessible forms, and
improper document formatting can create barriers that automated
tools often fail to detect. Ensuring accessibility requires a
combination of automated testing and human evaluation to
address complex issues like keyboard navigation, dynamic content,
and contextual readability. Organizations that prioritize
professional accessibility solutions not only enhance user
experience but also demonstrate a commitment to inclusivity,
making digital spaces more accessible for all users.

Ensuring Long-Term Web Accessibility: Challenges and Solutions

Web accessibility is not a one-time task but an ongoing commitment that requires continuous effort, monitoring, and adaptation. As technology evolves and digital content changes, organizations must proactively maintain accessibility to ensure compliance with evolving Web Content Accessibility Guidelines (WCAG) and legal requirements. Failure to do so can lead to usability challenges, legal risks, and reputational damage.

Challenges in Maintaining Web Accessibility

Many organizations struggle with ongoing accessibility due to various factors:

1. Frequent Website Updates

- New content, features, and design changes can inadvertently introduce accessibility issues.

- Without proper oversight, updates may break existing accessible elements, leading to non-compliance.

2. Emerging Technologies and Changing Standards

- Web accessibility guidelines evolve over time to address new challenges, requiring businesses to adapt.

- Staying compliant demands regular training, audits, and updates to development practices.

3. Lack of Internal Expertise

- Many organizations lack dedicated accessibility specialists, leading to accidental non-compliance.

- Without training, web developers and content creators may introduce inaccessible elements unknowingly.

4. Legal and Compliance Risks

- The rise in web accessibility lawsuits highlights the consequences of failing to maintain compliance.

- Non-compliance can result in legal penalties, financial losses, and reputational damage.

Best Practices for Maintaining Long-Term Accessibility

1. Stay Updated with WCAG and Accessibility Trends

- Follow trusted resources such as:

  - **Official Guidelines and Government Websites**: W3C Web Accessibility Initiative (WAI) (the official source for WCAG updates), U.S. Access Board (provides updates on accessibility regulations for digital content), and Section508.gov (offers guidance on accessibility standards for federal agencies and contractors), and

  - **Industry Publications and News Sources**: Accessibility.com (covers digital accessibility trends and best practices), Verbit's Accessibility Hub (tracks WCAG updates and shares implementation strategies), and UsableNet (provides expert insights on accessibility best practices).

- Engage with the Accessibility Community

  - **Join Professional Networks**: Participate in LinkedIn groups focused on accessibility, such as LinkedIn Accessibility Advice, and follow accessibility experts and advocacy organizations on social media.

- o **Attend Webinars and Conferences**: Register for events and training sessions hosted by W3C, Section508.gov, and industry leaders and engage with panels that discuss WCAG updates and real-world accessibility implementations.

2. Train and Educate Your Team

- Leverage Free and Official Training Resources:
  - o Section508.gov Training: In-depth courses on federal accessibility standards
  - o U.S. Access Board ICT Training: Offers guidance on making digital content accessible.
  - o 18F Accessibility Training Videos: Educates teams on best practices for inclusive design.
- Internal Training Programs:
  - o Host quarterly workshops for web developers, designers, and content creators.
  - o Include accessibility training in employee onboarding programs.
  - o Offer refresher courses when WCAG updates are released.
- Establish Clear Accessibility Roles:
  - o Designate an Accessibility Lead: Appoint a dedicated team member to oversee compliance and training efforts.
  - o Assign Accessibility Champions: Identify key team members across departments to promote best practices.

○ Foster Cross-Functional Collaboration: Encourage cooperation between developers, designers, content teams, and compliance officers.

3. Conduct Regular Accessibility Audits

- Automated Testing: Use tools like Axe, WAVE, and Lighthouse to identify issues.

- Manual Testing: Perform usability tests with individuals using assistive technologies.

- Routine Reviews: Schedule quarterly audits to ensure WCAG compliance.

4. Implement a Long-Term Accessibility Maintenance Plan

- Define Accessibility Goals: Establish measurable KPIs for compliance.

- Create an Accessibility Statement: Publicly outline your commitment to digital inclusion.

- Encourage User Feedback: Provide mechanisms for reporting accessibility concerns.

5. Hire a 508 remediation company to provide regular, consistent reviews of your website and documents.

Despite best efforts to maintain accessibility internally, many organizations face ongoing challenges due to limited expertise, resource constraints, and the complexity of evolving accessibility standards. While regular audits, training, and proactive planning can help mitigate risks, achieving and sustaining full compliance requires specialized knowledge and continuous oversight. For businesses struggling to keep pace with accessibility demands, outsourcing accessibility remediation offers a practical and efficient solution. By partnering with experienced professionals, organizations can ensure compliance, enhance user experience, and reduce the risk of legal and reputational consequences.

Benefits of Outsourcing Accessibility Remediation

1. Expertise and Specialization

- Professional vendors have in-depth knowledge of WCAG, ADA, Section 508, and other standards.

- They ensure precise remediation, addressing both obvious and nuanced accessibility barriers.

2. Efficiency and Time Savings

- Experts expedite the remediation process, allowing teams to focus on core business activities.

- Outsourcing eliminates the learning curve for accessibility best practices.

3. Risk Mitigation

- Compliance experts help prevent lawsuits and penalties by maintaining up-to-date standards.

- A professional approach reduces the likelihood of future accessibility failures.

Selecting the Right Accessibility Remediation Partner

When choosing an accessibility remediation service, consider the following key factors:

1. Comprehensive Service Offerings

- Website and document auditing for accessibility compliance.

- Remediation services, including content fixes and technical improvements.

- Ongoing monitoring to ensure long-term accessibility.

- Training programs to equip teams with accessibility best practices.

- It is beneficial to find a company that also provides accessible design services. This way they are able to modify documents to meet the ADA standards and streamline the process to accessibility. Accessibility practices are best implemented when integrated from the very beginning of each project.

2. Experience and Track Record

- Review client testimonials, case studies, and industry recognition to assess credibility.

- Ensure expertise in various content management systems (CMS) and document formats.

3. Balanced Testing Approaches

- Use both automated tools (e.g., Axe, WAVE) for efficiency and manual testing for accuracy.

- Validate assistive technology compatibility with screen readers like NVDA and JAWS.

4. Compliance with Current Standards

- Ensure adherence to WCAG 2.1 or higher and relevant legal requirements.

- Choose vendors who stay updated with accessibility laws and technological advancements.

5. Transparent Communication and Reporting

- Look for partners offering detailed reporting, clear project timelines, and post-remediation support.

- Ensure ongoing collaboration to maintain long-term accessibility compliance.

Fostering a Culture of Accessibility Within Your Organization

Regardless of your choice to outsource your web accessibility work, long-term accessibility is best achieved when it becomes an integral part of an organization's culture.

1. Secure Leadership Commitment

- Define clear accessibility goals aligned with company values.

- Allocate budget and resources for accessibility initiatives.

2. Integrate Accessibility into Business Processes

- Include accessibility reviews in project development and content workflows.

- Ensure internal digital tools are accessible for all employees.

3. Communicate Accessibility Efforts Externally

- Highlight achievements in digital accessibility through marketing and corporate communication.

- Engage in accessibility-focused events to showcase commitment and foster collaboration.

Conclusion

Maintaining web accessibility is an ongoing process that requires proactive monitoring, regular training, and a commitment to compliance with evolving standards. Organizations must address challenges such as frequent website updates, emerging technologies, and legal risks by integrating accessibility into their workflows, fostering a culture of inclusivity, and outsourcing to remediation experts. Regular audits, structured maintenance plans, and team education help sustain accessibility efforts while outsourcing to professional remediation services can enhance efficiency and ensure compliance. By prioritizing accessibility at every level, businesses can create a more inclusive digital environment, improve user experience, and mitigate legal and reputational risks.

Appendix – HHS 508 Accessibility Checklists

Adobe PDF

Guidelines	WCAG Ref #(s)	Failure Conditions
Best Practices	N/A	Document Properties > Description "Application" or "PDF Producer" does not display "Adobe LiveCycle Designer". (Please contact your Section 508 program team for guidance if the statement is false.)
	N/A	Document Properties > Security > "Content Copying for Accessibility" displays "Allowed", If the statement is false, the security settings must be updated.
	N/A	The Accessibility Full Check does not display "Scripts – Needs manual check" under the "Page Content" category. If the statement is false, a web and applications checklist is required to validate the content.
	N/A	Where no method exists to correct content so that it meets the requirements, an alternate version is provided. If the statement is false, contact your Section 508 program team for alternate content options.
	N/A	Where the document links to or embeds another file, an appropriate checklist has been provided for each link or attachment.

1.1 - Text Alternatives Non-Text Content	1.1.1	All images and form image buttons have appropriate, concise alternative text.
	1.1.1	Images that do not convey content, are decorative, or with content that is already conveyed in text are changed to artifacts.
	1.1.1	Equivalent alternatives to complex images are provided in context or on a separate (linked and/or referenced) page.
	1.1.1	Images of, or that include text (ex. logos), have the text as part of the description.
	1.1.1	Embedded multimedia is identified via accessible text.
	1.1.1	Animated content has an alternative or is described in text.
	1.1.1	Mathematical formulas have an alternatives or are provided as text.
1.2 - Time-based Media	1.1.1; 1.2.#	Where media content is present or embedded, the checkpoints on the Time-Based Media worksheet are compliant.
1.3 – Adaptable Info and Relationships; Parsing	1.3.1; 4.1.1	"Yes" is displayed next to "Tagged PDF" under Document Properties > Description > Advanced.
Info and Relationships; Name, Role, Value	1.3.1; 4.1.2	Tags are used to structure content in a valid manner (ex. a table is designated by a table tag).
	1.3.1; 4.1.2	Non-standard tags are mapped appropriately in the Role Map.
	1.3.1	Tags are used appropriately to designate headings (i.e. <H1> - <H6>).

1.3.1	Heading tags are provided in appropriate sequence (<H1>, <H2>, <H3>, etc.).
1.3.1	Tags are used appropriately to structure Table of Contents lists (<TOC>, <TOCI>).
1.3.1	Tags are used appropriately to structure lists (a minimum of <L> and <LI> are used).
1.3.1	Tags are used and nested appropriately to structure sub-lists (a minimum of <L> and <LI> are used).
1.3.1	Tables are used for tabular data.
1.3.1	Data table headers are appropriately identified (ex. TH for simple tables and the headers attribute for complex tables).
1.3.1	Data cells are associated with their headers (ex. scope for simple tables or headers and IDs for complex tables).
1.3.1	RowSpan or ColSpan is used appropriately for merged cells.
1.3.1	Data table captions and summaries are used where appropriate.
1.3.1	Tables are not used to construct layout. Where tables are used for layout purposes, and not data, all table tags are removed from the Tags structure.
1.3.1	Form input elements have tool tips that identify their purpose and match the associated text label.

	1.3.1	Related form elements and elements with multiple labels are grouped appropriately (ex. group name is identified as part of the tool tip of the element; radio buttons have the same name).
Meaningful Sequence	1.3.2	The reading and navigation order (determined by Show/Hide > Navigation Panes > Tags) is logical and intuitive.
	1.3.2	All meaningful content appears in the Tags pane.
	1.3.3	Vital content from a header, footer or watermark is provided in the document.
	1.3.4	Content that is repetitive or decorative is changed to an artifact.
Sensory Characteristics	1.3.3	Instructions do not rely upon shape, size, or visual location (e.g., "Click the square icon to continue" or "Instructions are in the right-hand column").
	1.3.3	Instructions do not rely upon sound (e.g., "A beeping sound indicates you may continue.").
1.4 – Distinguishable Use of Color	1.4.1	Color is not used as the sole method of conveying content or distinguishing visual elements.

	1.4.1	Color is not used as the sole method to distinguish links from surrounding text unless the luminance contrast between the link and the surrounding text is at least 3:1 and an additional differentiation (e.g., it becomes underlined) is provided when the link is hovered over or receives focus.
	1.4.1	Non-text content (ex. images) use patterns to convey the same information as color.
Audio Control	1.4.2	A mechanism is provided to stop, pause, mute, or adjust volume for audio from multimedia or animation that automatically plays for more than 3 seconds.
Contrast (Minimum)	1.4.3	Text and images of text have a contrast ratio of at least 4.5:1.
Resize Text	1.4.4	The document is readable and functional when the text is set to re-flow.
Images of Text	1.4.5	The "Scanned Page Alert" does not appear when the document is opened and the Tools > Accessibility > Full Check > "Document" category does not say "Failed" for "Image-only PDF" or "Tagged PDF".
2.1 - Keyboard Accessible Keyboard	2.1.1	All document functionality is available (receive focus and can be activated) using the keyboard, unless the functionality cannot be accomplished in any known way using a keyboard (e.g., free hand drawing).

	2.1.1	All functionality of the content is operable without requiring specific timings for individual keystrokes.
Info and Relationships; Keyboard; Name, Role, Value	1.3.1; 2.1.1; 4.1.2	Links are properly structured using the <Link> tag with a nested <Link-OBJR> tag.
No Keyboard Trap	2.1.2	Keyboard focus is never locked or trapped at one particular page element. The user can navigate to and from all navigable page elements (ex. embedded objects) using only a keyboard.
2.2 - Enough Time Timing Adjustable	2.2.1	If a page or application has a time limit, the user is given options to turn off, adjust, or extend that time limit. This is not a requirement for real-time events (e.g., an auction), where the time limit is absolutely required, or if the time limit is longer than 20 hours.
Pause, Stop, Hide	2.2.2	Automatically moving, blinking, scrolling, or auto-updating content (ex. multimedia, animation, dynamic content, etc.) that lasts longer than 5 seconds can be paused, stopped, or hidden by the user. Moving, blinking, or scrolling can be used to draw attention to or highlight content as long as it lasts less than 5 seconds.
2.3 – Seizures Three Flashes or Below Threshold	2.3.1	No page content flashes more than 3 times per second unless that flashing content is sufficiently small and the flashes are of low contrast and do not contain too much red.

2.4 - Navigable Page Titles	2.4.2	The document has a meaningful title indicating its purpose under Document Properties > Description > "Title" and Document Properties > Initial View > Window Options > Show is set to "Document Title".
Keyboard; Focus Order	2.1.1; 2.4.3	The navigation order of links, form elements, etc. is logical and intuitive.
	2.4.3	Keyboard focus moves to and returns from elements appropriately (ex. the opening or appearance and closing of dialogs).
Link Purpose (In Context)	2.4.4	The purpose of each link (or form image button) can be determined from the link text alone, or from the link text and its context (e.g., surrounding paragraph, list item, table cell, or table headers).
	2.4.4	Links (or form image buttons) with the same text that go to different locations are readily distinguishable.
Headings and Labels	2.4.6	Page headings and labels for form and interactive controls are informative. Avoid duplicating headings (e.g., "More Details") or label text (e.g., "First Name") unless the structure provides adequate differentiation between them.
Focus Visible	2.4.7	It is visually apparent which element has the current keyboard focus (i.e., as you tab through the page, you can see where you are).

3.1 – Readable Language of Page	3.1.1	Document Properties > Advanced > Reading Options > Language displays the appropriate language for the document.
Language of Parts	3.1.2	The language of page content that is in a different language is identified through the Properties of the affected tag(s) under the Tag tab > Language.
3.2 – Predictable On Focus	3.2.1	When a page element receives focus, it does not result in a substantial change to the page, the spawning of a pop-up window, an additional change of keyboard focus, or any other change that could confuse or disorient the user.
On Input	3.2.2	When a user inputs information or interacts with a control, it does not result in a substantial change to the page, the spawning of a pop-up window, an additional change of keyboard focus, or any other change that could confuse or disorient the user unless the user is informed of the change ahead of time.
3.3 - Input Assistance Error Identification Labels or Instructions	3.3.1; 3.3.2	Required form elements or form elements that require a specific format, value, or length provide this information as a text description.

	3.3.1	If utilized, form validation errors are presented in an efficient, intuitive, and accessible manner. The error is clearly identified, quick access to the problematic element is provided, and user is allowed to easily fix the error and resubmit the form.
Labels or Instructions	3.3.2	Sufficient labels, cues, and instructions for required interactive elements are provided at the beginning of the form or set of fields via instructions, examples, and/or properly positioned form labels. Note: Related fields need to provide a group name, example "Gender: Female".
Error Suggestion	3.3.3	If an input error is detected, provide suggestions for fixing the input in a timely and accessible manner.
Error Prevention (Legal, Financial, Data)	3.3.4	If the user can change or delete legal, financial, or test data, the changes/deletions can be reversed, verified, or confirmed.

Microsoft Excel

Guidelines	WCAG Ref #(s)	Failure Conditions
Best Practices	N/A	Where no method exists to correct content so that it meets the requirements, an alternate version is provided. If the statement is false, contact your Section 508 program team for alternate content options.

	N/A	Where the document links to or embeds another file, an appropriate checklist has been provided for each link or attachment.
1.1 - Text Alternatives Non-Text Content	1.1.1	All images/objects/shapes have descriptive text alt text (Format Picture > Layout & Properties > Alt Text > Description), a caption, or are described in the surrounding text.
	1.1.1	Images that do not convey content, are decorative, or with content that is already conveyed in text have a blank space in the Format Picture > Layout & Properties > Alt Text > Description field. (Note: When using Office 365, check the "Mark as Decorative" checkbox instead.)
	1.1.1	Equivalent alternatives to complex images are provided in context or on a separate worksheet.
	1.1.1	Images of, or that include text (ex. logos), have the text as part of the description.
	1.1.1	Embedded content is identified via accessible text.
	1.1.1	Animated content has an alternative or is described in text.
	1.1.1	Mathematical formulas (symbols outside the common set) have an alternative or are provided as text.
	1.1.1	All characters are Unicode values.
	1.1.1	Images and drawing remnants are grouped where appropriate.

1.2 - Time-based Media	1.1.1; 1.2.#	Where media content is present or embedded, the checkpoints on the Time-Based Media worksheet are compliant.
1.3 – Adaptable Info and Relationships; Name, Role, Value	1.3.1; 4.1.2	Blank lines, tabs or spaces are not used for structure.
	1.3.1	The use of text boxes is avoided where possible.
	1.3.1	Home > Style > Heading 1 - Heading 4 are used to style section names.
	1.3.1	Headings match the visual hierarchy of the document.
	1.3.1	Insert > Table function is used for tabular data and merged or split cells are avoided.
	1.3.1	Data table headers are appropriately identified by checking the "My table has headers" checkbox in the Create Table dialog.
	1.3.1	Data table row and column header cells are not blank.
	1.3.1	Data table row and/or column headers are repeated at the top of each page by ensuring applicable rows and/or columns are listed under Page Layout > Print Titles > Page Setup > Sheet > Print titles.
	1.3.1; 4.1.2	The document is free of pictures of tables.
	1.3.1	Data table captions and summaries are used where appropriate.
	1.3.1; 4.1.2	Form elements are avoided where possible.

Meaningful Sequence	1.3.2	The reading and navigation order is logical and intuitive.
	1.3.2	Vital content from a header, footer or watermark is duplicated near the beginning of the document.
Sensory Characteristics	1.3.3	Instructions do not rely upon shape, size, or visual location (e.g., "Click the square icon to continue" or "Instructions are in the right-hand column").
	1.3.3	Instructions do not rely upon sound (e.g., "A beeping sound indicates you may continue.").
1.4 – Distinguishable Use of Color	1.4.1	Color is not used as the sole method of conveying content or distinguishing visual elements (such as size, shape, and location).
	1.4.1	Color alone is not used to distinguish links from surrounding text unless the luminance contrast between the link and the surrounding text is at least 3:1 and an additional differentiation (e.g., it becomes underlined) is provided when the link is hovered over or receives focus.
	1.4.1	Non-text content (ex. images) use patterns to convey the same information as color.
	1.4.1	Comments are used as collaboration methods (instead of color and highlighting).
Audio Control	1.4.2	A mechanism is provided to stop, pause, mute, or adjust volume for audio from multimedia or animation that automatically plays for more than 3 seconds.

Contrast (Minimum)	1.4.3	Text and images of text have a contrast ratio of at least 4.5:1.
Resize Text	1.4.4	The document is readable and functional when the text is resized up to 200 percent.
Images of Text	1.4.5	Text is used instead of images of text (unless it is essential for conveying the information).
2.1 - Keyboard Accessible Keyboard	2.1.1	All document functionality is available (receives focus and can be activated) using the keyboard, unless the functionality cannot be accomplished in any known way using a keyboard (e.g., free hand drawing).
	2.1.1	All locked and unlocked cells must be capable of being selected and navigated with the keyboard. Navigate to Review > Protect Sheet for each worksheet and ensure "Select Locked Cells" and "Select Unlocked Cells" are checked.
	2.1.1	All functionality of the content is operable without requiring specific timings for individual keystrokes.
No Keyboard Trap	2.1.2	Keyboard focus is never locked or trapped at one particular document element. The user can navigate to and from all navigable elements (ex. embedded objects) using only a keyboard.

2.2 - Enough Time Timing Adjustable	2.2.1	Where the application has a time limit, the user is given options to turn off, adjust, or extend that time limit. This is not a requirement for real-time events (e.g., an auction), where the time limit is absolutely required, or if the time limit is longer than 20 hours.
Pause, Stop, Hide	2.2.2	Automatically moving, blinking, scrolling, or auto-updating content (ex. multimedia, animation, etc.) that lasts longer than 5 seconds can be paused, stopped, or hidden by the user. Moving, blinking, or scrolling can be used to draw attention to or highlight content as long as it lasts less than 5 seconds.
2.3 – Seizures Three Flashes or Below Threshold	2.3.1	No page content flashes more than 3 times per second unless that flashing content is sufficiently small and the flashes are of low contrast and do not contain too much red.
2.4 - Navigable Page Titles	2.4.2	The document has a meaningful title indicating its purpose under File > Info > Properties > Title.
Keyboard; Focus Order	2.1.1; 2.4.3	The navigation order of links is logical and intuitive.
Link Purpose (In Context)	2.4.4	The destination, function, and/or purpose of each link can be determined from the link text alone, or from the link text and its context (e.g., surrounding paragraph, list item, table cell, or table headers).

	2.4.4	Links with the same text that go to different locations are readily distinguishable.
Headings and Labels	2.4.6	Page headings and labels for forms are informative. Avoid duplicating headings (e.g., "More Details") or label text (e.g., "First Name") unless the structure provides adequate differentiation between them.
	2.4.6	Each worksheet in the workbook has a meaningful, unique name.
Focus Visible	2.4.7	It is visually apparent which element has the current keyboard focus (i.e., as you tab through the page, you can see where you are).
3.1 – Readable Language of Page	3.1.1	File > Options > Language displays the appropriate language for the document.
3.2 – Predictable On Focus	3.2.1	When a page element receives focus, it does not result in a substantial change to the page, the spawning of a pop-up window, an additional change of keyboard focus, or any other change that could confuse or disorient the user.
On Input	3.2.2	When a user inputs information or interacts with a control, it does not result in a substantial change to the page, the spawning of a pop-up window, an additional change of keyboard focus, or any other change that could confuse or disorient the user unless the user is informed of the change ahead of time.

3.3 - Input Assistance Error Identification Labels or Instructions	3.3.1; 3.3.2	Required form elements or form elements that require a specific format, value, or length provide this information as a text description.
	3.3.1	If utilized, form validation errors are presented in an efficient, intuitive, and accessible manner. The error is clearly identified, quick access to the problematic element is provided, and user is allowed to easily fix the error and resubmit the form.
Labels or Instructions	3.3.2	Sufficient labels, cues, and instructions for required interactive elements are provided at the beginning of the form or set of fields via instructions, examples, and/or properly positioned form labels. Note: Related fields need to provide a group name, example "Gender: Female".
Error Suggestion	3.3.3	If an input error is detected, provide suggestions for fixing the input in a timely and accessible manner.
Error Prevention (Legal, Financial, Data)	3.3.4	If the user can change or delete legal, financial, or test data, the changes/deletions can be reversed, verified, or confirmed.

Microsoft PowerPoint

Guidelines	WCAG Ref #(s)	Failure Conditions
Best Practices	N/A	Where no method exists to correct content so that it meets the requirements, an alternate version is provided. If the statement is false, contact your Section 508 program team for alternate content options.
	N/A	Where the document links to or embeds another file, an appropriate checklist has been provided for each link or attachment.
1.1 - Text Alternatives Non-Text Content	1.1.1	All images/objects/shapes have descriptive text as alt text (Format Picture > Layout & Properties > Alt Text > Description), a caption, or are described in the surrounding text.
	1.1.1	Images that do not convey content, are decorative, or with content that is already conveyed in text have a blank space in the Format Picture > Layout & Properties > Alt Text > Description field. (Note: When using Office 365, check the "Mark as Decorative" checkbox instead.)
	1.1.1	Equivalent alternatives to complex images are provided in context or on a separate (linked and/or referenced) page.
	1.1.1	Images of, or that include text (ex. logos), have the text as part of the description.

	1.1.1	Embedded content (ex. Excel objects) is identified via accessible text.
	1.1.1	Animated content has an alternative or is described in text.
	1.1.1	Mathematical formulas have an alternatives or are provided as text.
	1.1.1	All characters are Unicode values.
	1.1.1	Images and drawing remnants are grouped where appropriate.
1.2 - Time-based Media	1.1.1; 1.2.#	Where media content is present or embedded, the checkpoints on the Time-Based Media worksheet are compliant.
1.3 – Adaptable Info and Relationships; Name, Role, Value	1.3.1; 4.1.2	Blank lines, tabs or spaces are not used for structure.
	1.3.1	Home > Arrange > Selection Pane displays Title and Subtitle objects for slide title elements.
	1.3.1	The bullets. numbering or multi-level list icon is selected on Home > Paragraph for all list items.
	1.3.1	A different bullet or numbering style (than the parent style) is selected for sub-list items.
	1.3.1	Insert > Table function is used for tabular data and merged or split cells are avoided.
	1.3.1	Data table headers are appropriately identified by the "Header Row" checkbox being checked under Tables > Design.
	1.3.1	Data table row and column header cells are not blank.

	1.3.1; 4.1.2	The presentation is free of pictures of tables.
	1.3.1	Data table captions and summaries are used where appropriate.
	1.3.1	When a layout table is used to provide structure, the "tab" order follows the visually implied reading order.
Meaningful Sequence	1.3.2	Home > Arrange > Selection Pane displays the slide content (including multiple columns) from bottom to top in the visually implied reading order.
Non-Text Content; Meaningful Sequence	1.1.1; 1.3.2	Vital header, footer or background content is duplicated from View > Slide Master near the beginning of the presentation.
	1.3.2	Additional content that has been placed in the Slide Notes is identified on the slide itself or at the beginning of the presentation.
Sensory Characteristics	1.3.3	Instructions do not rely upon shape, size, or visual location (e.g., "Click the square icon to continue" or "Instructions are in the right-hand column").
	1.3.3	Instructions do not rely upon sound (e.g., "A beeping sound indicates you may continue").
1.4 – Distinguishable Use of Color	1.4.1	Color is not used as the sole method of conveying content or distinguishing visual elements (such as size, shape, and location).

	1.4.1	Color alone is not used to distinguish links from surrounding text unless the luminance contrast between the link and the surrounding text is at least 3:1 and an additional differentiation (e.g., it becomes underlined) is provided when the link is hovered over or receives focus.
	1.4.1	Non-text content (ex. images) use patterns to convey the same information as color.
	1.4.1	Comments are used as collaboration methods (instead of color and highlighting).
Audio Control	1.4.2	A mechanism is provided to stop, pause, mute, or adjust volume for audio from multimedia or animation that automatically plays for more than 3 seconds.
Contrast (Minimum)	1.4.3	Text and images of text have a contrast ratio of at least 4.5:1.
Resize Text	1.4.4	The document is readable and functional when the text is resized up to 200 percent.
Images of Text	1.4.5	Text is used instead of images of text (unless it is essential for conveying the information).
2.1 - Keyboard Accessible Keyboard	2.1.1	All document functionality is available (receives focus and can be activated) using the keyboard, unless the functionality cannot be accomplished in any known way using a keyboard (e.g., free hand drawing).

	2.1.1	All functionality of the content is operable without requiring specific timings for individual keystrokes.
No Keyboard Trap	2.1.2	Keyboard focus is never locked or trapped at one particular document element. The user can navigate to and from all navigable elements (ex. embedded objects) using only a keyboard.
2.2 - Enough Time Timing Adjustable	2.2.1	Where the application has a time limit, the user is given options to turn off, adjust, or extend that time limit. This is not a requirement for real-time events (e.g., an auction), where the time limit is absolutely required, or if the time limit is longer than 20 hours.
Pause, Stop, Hide	2.2.2	Automatically moving, blinking, scrolling, or auto-updating content (ex. multimedia, animation, etc.) that lasts longer than 5 seconds can be paused, stopped, or hidden by the user. Moving, blinking, or scrolling can be used to draw attention to or highlight content as long as it lasts less than 5 seconds.
	2.2.2	Slides only advance via mouse click (Transitions > Timing > Advance Slides > On Mouse Click is checked).
2.3 – Seizures Three Flashes or Below Threshold	2.3.1	No page content flashes more than 3 times per second unless that flashing content is sufficiently small and the flashes are of low contrast and do not contain too much red.

2.4 - Navigable Page Titles	2.4.2	The presentation has a meaningful title indicating its purpose under File > Info > Properties > Title.
Keyboard; Focus Order	2.1.1; 2.4.3	The navigation order of links, buttons, etc. is logical and intuitive.
Link Purpose (In Context)	2.4.4	The destination, function, and/or purpose of each link (or form image button) can be determined from the link text alone, or from the link text and its context (e.g., surrounding paragraph, list item, table cell, or table headers).
	2.4.4	Links (or form image buttons) with the same text that go to different locations are readily distinguishable.
Headings and Labels	2.4.6	Slide titles are unique and informative. Avoid duplicating slide titles unless the structure provides adequate differentiation between them.
Focus Visible	2.4.7	It is visually apparent which element has the current keyboard focus (i.e., as you tab through the page, you can see where you are).
3.1 – Readable Language of Page	3.1.1	Review > Language > Language Preferences displays the appropriate language for the presentation.
Language of Parts	3.1.2	The language of slide content that is in a different language is identified through Review > Language > Set Proofing Language.
3.2 – Predictable On Focus; On Input; Name, Role, Value	3.2.1; 3.2.2; 4.1.2	Form controls and quizzes are not present unless an equivalent alternative is provided.

3.3 - Input Assistance Error Identification; Labels or Instructions	3.3.1; 3.3.2	Errors and instructions are provided at the beginning of the slide content via cues, examples, and/or properly positioned labels.
Error Suggestion	3.3.3	If an input error is detected, provide suggestions for fixing the input in a timely and accessible manner.
Error Prevention (Legal, Financial, Data)	3.3.4	If the user can change or delete legal, financial, or test data, the changes/deletions can be reversed, verified, or confirmed.
4.1 – Compatible Name, Role, Value	4.1.2	Links are inserted using the hyperlink dialog and the raw URL is provided somewhere (on the same slide, in the slide notes or in an appendix slide) so that users of assistive technology can access the content.

Microsoft Word

Guidelines	WCAG Ref #(s)	Failure Conditions
Best Practices	N/A	Where no method exists to correct content so that it meets the requirements, an alternate version is provided. If the statement is false, contact your Section 508 program team for alternate content options.
	N/A	Where the document links to or embeds another file, an appropriate checklist has been provided for each link or attachment.

1.1 - Text Alternatives Non-Text Content	1.1.1	All images/objects/shapes have descriptive text as alt text (Format Picture > Layout & Properties > Alt Text > Description), a caption, or are described in the surrounding text.
	1.1.1	Images that do not convey content, are decorative, or with content that is already conveyed in text have a blank space in the Format Picture > Layout & Properties > Alt Text > Description field. (Note: When using Office 365, check the "Mark as Decorative" checkbox instead.)
	1.1.1	Equivalent alternatives to complex images are provided in context or on a separate (linked and/or referenced) page.
	1.1.1	Images of, or that include text (ex. logos), have the text as part of the description.
	1.1.1	All images or objects in the document have the Text Wrap (Format > Wrap Text) property set to In Line with Text.
	1.1.1	Embedded content (ex. Excel objects) is identified via accessible text.
	1.1.1	Animated content has an alternative or is described in text.
	1.1.1	Mathematical formulas have an alternatives or are provided as text.
	1.1.1	All characters are Unicode values.
	1.1.1	Images and drawing remnants are grouped where appropriate.

1.2 - Time-based Media	1.1.1; 1.2.#	Where media content is present or embedded, the checkpoints on the Time-Based Media worksheet are compliant.
1.3 – Adaptable Info and Relationships; Name, Role, Value	1.3.1; 4.1.2	Blank lines, tabs or spaces are not used for structure.
	1.3.1	The use of text boxes is avoided where possible. If text boxes must be used, Text Wrap is set to In Line with Text.
	1.3.1	View > Navigation Pane > Headings shows all the headings visually seen in the document.
	1.3.1	View > Navigation Pane > Headings matches the visual hierarchy of the document.
	1.3.1	When a table of content is present, an "Automatic Table" option is selected from the Reference > Table of Contents menu.
	1.3.1	The bullets. numbering or multi-level list icon is selected on Home > Paragraph for all list items.
	1.3.1	A different bullet or numbering style (than the parent style) is selected for sub-list items.
	1.3.1	Insert > Table function is used for tabular data and merged or split cells are avoided.
	1.3.1	Data table headers are appropriately identified by ensuring "Header Row" is checked under Table Tools > Design and for tables spanning multiple pages "Repeat as Header Row" is checked in table properties.

	1.3.1	Data table row and column header cells are not blank.
	1.3.1; 4.1.2	The document is free of pictures of tables.
	1.3.1	Data table captions and summaries are used where appropriate.
	1.3.1	When a layout table is used to provide structure, the "tab" order follows the visually implied reading order.
	1.3.1	For a layout or data table, Table Properties > Text Wrapping is set to none.
	1.3.1; 4.1.2	Form input elements are within protected sections of the document.
	1.3.1; 4.1.2	Descriptive on-screen labels are provided for each form element.
	1.3.1	Related form elements and elements with multiple labels are grouped appropriately (ex. group name is identified as part of the tool tip of the element; radio buttons have the same name).
Meaningful Sequence	1.3.2	The reading and navigation order is logical and intuitive.
	1.3.2	All content that visually appears in columns is structured properly using the Layout > Columns feature. (The Reveal Formatting pane (Shift + F1) > Section can also be used to determine this. If Columns is listed for columned content then it is correct.)

	1.3.2	Vital content from a header, footer or watermark is duplicated near the beginning of the document.
Sensory Characteristics	1.3.3	Instructions do not rely upon shape, size, or visual location (e.g., "Click the square icon to continue" or "Instructions are in the right-hand column").
	1.3.3	Instructions do not rely upon sound (e.g., "A beeping sound indicates you may continue").
1.4 – Distinguishable Use of Color	1.4.1	Color is not used as the sole method of conveying content or distinguishing visual elements (such as size, shape, and location).
	1.4.1	Color alone is not used to distinguish links from surrounding text unless the luminance contrast between the link and the surrounding text is at least 3:1 and an additional differentiation (e.g., it becomes underlined) is provided when the link is hovered over or receives focus.
	1.4.1	Non-text content (ex. images) use patterns to convey the same information as color.
	1.4.1	Comments and Track Changes are used as collaboration methods (instead of color and highlighting).
Audio Control	1.4.2	A mechanism is provided to stop, pause, mute, or adjust volume for audio from multimedia or animation that automatically plays for more than 3 seconds.
Contrast (Minimum)	1.4.3	Text and images of text have a contrast ratio of at least 4.5:1.

Resize Text	1.4.4	The document is readable and functional when the text is resized up to 200 percent.
Images of Text	1.4.5	Text is used instead of images of text (unless it is essential for conveying the information).
2.1 - Keyboard Accessible Keyboard	2.1.1	All document functionality is available (receives focus and can be activated) using the keyboard, unless the functionality cannot be accomplished in any known way using a keyboard (e.g., free hand drawing).
	2.1.1	Review > Restrict Editing, the "Stop Protection" button does not appear at the bottom of the Restrict Editing pane. (Exception: If there are fillable form fields and sections to the document, then enforcing protection is appropriate.)
	2.1.1	All functionality of the content is operable without requiring specific timings for individual keystrokes.
	2.1.1	Content, other than fillable form elements, is available in unprotected sections of the document.
No Keyboard Trap	2.1.2	Keyboard focus is never locked or trapped at one particular document element. The user can navigate to and from all navigable elements (ex. embedded objects) using only a keyboard.

2.2 - Enough Time Timing Adjustable	2.2.1	Where the application has a time limit, the user is given options to turn off, adjust, or extend that time limit. This is not a requirement for real-time events (e.g., an auction), where the time limit is absolutely required, or if the time limit is longer than 20 hours.
Pause, Stop, Hide	2.2.2	Automatically moving, blinking, scrolling, or auto updating content (ex. multimedia, animation, etc.) that lasts longer than 5 seconds can be paused, stopped, or hidden by the user. Moving, blinking, or scrolling can be used to draw attention to or highlight content as long as it lasts less than 5 seconds.
2.3 – Seizures Three Flashes or Below Threshold	2.3.1	No page content flashes more than 3 times per second unless that flashing content is sufficiently small and the flashes are of low contrast and do not contain too much red.
2.4 – Navigable Page Titles	2.4.2	The document has a meaningful title indicating its purpose under File > Info > Properties > Title.
Keyboard; Focus Order	2.1.1; 2.4.3	The navigation order of links, form elements, etc. is logical and intuitive.
Link Purpose (In Context)	2.4.4	The destination, function, and/or purpose of each link (or form image button) can be determined from the link text alone, or from the link text and its context (e.g., surrounding paragraph, list item, table cell, or table headers).

	2.4.4	Links (or form image buttons) with the same text that go to different locations are readily distinguishable.
Headings and Labels	2.4.6	Page headings and labels for form and interactive controls are informative. Avoid duplicating headings (e.g., "More Details") or label text (e.g., "First Name") unless the structure provides adequate differentiation between them.
Focus Visible	2.4.7	It is visually apparent which element has the current keyboard focus (i.e., as you tab through the page, you can see where you are).
3.1 – Readable Language of Page	3.1.1	The Reveal Formatting pane (Shift + F1) > Font > Language displays the appropriate language for the document.
Language of Parts	3.1.2	The language of page content that is in a different language is identified through Review > Language > Set Proofing Language.
3.2 – Predictable On Focus	3.2.1	When a page element receives focus, it does not result in a substantial change to the page, the spawning of a pop-up window, an additional change of keyboard focus, or any other change that could confuse or disorient the user.

On Input	3.2.2	When a user inputs information or interacts with a control, it does not result in a substantial change to the page, the spawning of a pop-up window, an additional change of keyboard focus, or any other change that could confuse or disorient the user unless the user is informed of the change ahead of time.
3.3 - Input Assistance Error Identification Labels or Instructions	3.3.1; 3.3.2	Required form elements or form elements that require a specific format, value, or length provide this information as a text description.
	3.3.1	If utilized, form validation errors are presented in an efficient, intuitive, and accessible manner. The error is clearly identified, quick access to the problematic element is provided, and user is allowed to easily fix the error and resubmit the form.
Labels or Instructions	3.3.2	Sufficient labels, cues, and instructions for required interactive elements are provided at the beginning of the form or set of fields via instructions, examples, and/or properly positioned form labels. Note: Related fields need to provide a group name, example "Gender: Female".
Error Suggestion	3.3.3	If an input error is detected, provide suggestions for fixing the input in a timely and accessible manner.

Error Prevention (Legal, Financial, Data)	3.3.4	If the user can change or delete legal, financial, or test data, the changes/deletions can be reversed, verified, or confirmed.
4.1 – Compatible Name, Role, Value	4.1.2	Only Legacy Form controls are used from Developer > Controls for interactive form elements.

Web Sites, Web Applications, & Software

Guidelines	WCAG Ref #(s)	Failure Conditions
Best Practices	N/A	Where no method exists to correct content so that it meets the requirements, an alternate version is provided. If the statement is false, contact your Section 508 program team for alternate content options.
	N/A	Where the document links to or embeds another file, an appropriate checklist has been provided for each link or attachment.
1.1 - Text Alternatives Non-Text Content	1.1.1	All images, form image buttons, and image map hot spots have appropriate, concise alternative text.
	1.1.1	Images that do not convey content, are decorative, or with content that is already conveyed in text are given null alt text (alt="") or implemented as CSS backgrounds.
	1.1.1	Equivalent alternatives to complex images are provided in context or on a separate (linked and/or referenced via longdesc) page.

	1.1.1	Embedded multimedia is identified via accessible text.
	1.1.1	Frames are appropriately titled.
	1.1.1	Content intended to be hidden from all users is also hidden from assistive technology.
	1.1.1	CSS background images that convey meaning have textual alternatives.
	1.1.1	Animated content has an alternative or is described in text.
	1.1.1	CAPTCHAs are accessible, in visual and audible formats.
	1.1.1	Textual alternative information is updated when an element's state changes.
1.2 - Time-based Media	1.1.1; 1.2.#	Where media content is present or embedded, the checkpoints on the Time-Based Media worksheet are compliant.
1.3 - Adaptable Info and Relationships	1.3.1	Semantic markup is used appropriately to designate headings (<h1>), lists (<ul>, <ol>, and <dl>), emphasized or special text (<strong>, <code>, <abbr>, <blockquote>, for example), etc.
	1.3.1	Tables are used for tabular data and data is contained in separate data cells.
	1.3.1	Data table headers are appropriately identified (ex. TH for simple tables and the headers attribute for complex tables).

	1.3.1	Data cells are associated with their headers (ex. scope for simple tables or headers and IDs for complex tables).
	1.3.1	Data table captions and summaries are used where appropriate.
	1.3.1	Layout tables identify their purpose and do not contain structural markup.
	1.3.1	Text labels are associated with form input elements.
	1.3.1	Related form elements are grouped with fieldset/legend.
	1.3.1	Elements with multiple labels are provided in a meaningful order.
Meaningful Sequence	1.3.2	The reading and navigation order (determined by code order) is logical and intuitive.
	1.3.2	Meaningful CSS content must be available and in a logical order when viewed without style sheets.
	1.3.2	Menus, simulated dialogs, calendar pickers, and dynamic content are rendered inline with the controls that spawn them.
Sensory Characteristics	1.3.3	Instructions do not rely upon shape, size, or visual location (e.g., "Click the square icon to continue" or "Instructions are in the right-hand column").
	1.3.3	Instructions do not rely upon sound (e.g., "A beeping sound indicates you may continue").
1.4 - Distinguishable Use of Color	1.4.1	Color is not used as the sole method of conveying content or distinguishing visual elements.

	1.4.1	Color alone is not used to distinguish links from surrounding text unless the luminance contrast between the link and the surrounding text is at least 3:1 and an additional differentiation (e.g., it becomes underlined) is provided when the link is hovered over or receives focus.
	1.4.1	Non-text content (ex. images) use patterns to convey the same information as color.
Audio Control	1.4.2	A mechanism is provided to stop, pause, mute, or adjust volume for audio from multimedia or animation that automatically plays in software for more than 3 seconds.
Contrast (Minimum)	1.4.3	Text and images of text have a contrast ratio of at least 4.5:1.
Resize Text	1.4.4	The page is readable and functional when the text size is doubled.
Images of Text	1.4.5	If the same visual presentation can be made using text alone, an image is not used to present that text.
2.1 - Keyboard Accessible Keyboard	2.1.1	All page functionality is available using the keyboard, unless the functionality cannot be accomplished in any known way using a keyboard (e.g., free hand drawing).
	2.1.1	Page-specified shortcut keys and accesskeys (accesskey should typically be avoided) do not conflict with existing browser and screen reader shortcuts.

	2.1.1	All functionality of the content is operable without requiring specific timings for individual keystrokes.
	2.1.1	Device-dependent event handlers are avoided.
No Keyboard Trap	2.1.2	Keyboard focus is never locked or trapped at one particular page element. The user can navigate to and from all navigable page elements (ex. embedded objects) using only a keyboard.
2.2 - Enough Time Timing Adjustable	2.2.1	If a page or application has a time limit, the user is given options to turn off, adjust, or extend that time limit. This is not a requirement for real-time events (e.g., an auction), where the time limit is absolutely required, or if the time limit is longer than 20 hours.
Pause, Stop, Hide	2.2.2	Automatically moving, blinking, or scrolling content (ex. multimedia, animation, etc.) that lasts longer than 5 seconds can be paused, stopped, or hidden by the user. Moving, blinking, or scrolling can be used to draw attention to or highlight content as long as it lasts less than 5 seconds.
	2.2.2	Automatically updating content (e.g., automatically redirecting or refreshing a page, a news ticker, AJAX updated field, a notification alert, etc.) can be paused, stopped, or hidden by the user or the user can manually control the timing of the updates.

2.3 - Seizures Three Flashes or Below Threshold	2.3.1	No page content flashes more than 3 times per second unless that flashing content is sufficiently small and the flashes are of low contrast and do not contain too much red. (See general flash and red flash thresholds.)
2.4 - Navigable Bypass Blocks (2.4.1 Does not apply to software.)	2.4.1	A link is provided to skip navigation and other page elements that are repeated across web pages.
	2.4.1	If a page has a proper heading structure, this may be considered a sufficient technique instead of a "Skip to main content" link.
	2.4.1	If a page uses frames and the frames are appropriately titled, this is a sufficient technique for bypassing individual frames.
Page Titles	2.4.2	The web page has a descriptive and informative page title.
Focus Order	2.4.3	The navigation order of links, form elements, etc. is logical and intuitive.
	2.4.3	Keyboard focus moves to and returns from elements appropriately. This includes the opening or appearance and closing of menus, dialogs, calendars, etc.
Link Purpose (In Context)	2.4.4	The purpose of each link (or form image button or image map hotspot) can be determined from the link text alone, or from the link text and its context (e.g., surrounding paragraph, list item, table cell, or table headers).

	2.4.4	Links (or form image buttons) with the same text that go to different locations are readily distinguishable.
Multiple Ways (2.4.5 Does not apply to software.)	2.4.5	Multiple ways are available to find other web pages on the site - at least two of: a list of related pages, table of contents, site map, site search, or list of all available web pages.
Headings and Labels	2.4.6	Page headings and labels for form and interactive controls are informative. Avoid duplicating heading (e.g., "More Details") or label text (e.g., "First Name") unless the structure provides adequate differentiation between them.
Focus Visible	2.4.7	It is visually apparent which page element has the current keyboard focus (i.e., as you tab through the page, you can see where you are).
3.1 – Readable Language of Page	3.1.1	The language of the page is identified using the HTML lang attribute (<html lang="en">, for example).
Language of Parts	3.1.2	The language of page content that is in a different language is identified using the lang attribute (e.g., <blockquote lang="es">).
3.2 – Predictable On Focus	3.2.1	When a page element receives focus, it does not result in a substantial change to the page, the spawning of a pop-up window, an additional change of keyboard focus, or any other change that could confuse or disorient the user.

On Input	3.2.2	When a user inputs information or interacts with a control, it does not result in a substantial change to the page, the spawning of a pop-up window, an additional change of keyboard focus, or any other change that could confuse or disorient the user unless the user is informed of the change ahead of time.
Consistent Navigation (3.2.3 Does not apply to software.)	3.2.3	Navigation links that are repeated on web pages do not change order when navigating through the site.
Consistent Identification (3.2.4 Does not apply to software.)	3.2.4	Elements that have the same functionality across multiple web pages are consistently identified. For example, a search box at the top of the site should always be labeled the same way.
3.3 - Input Assistance Error Identification	3.3.1	Required form elements or form elements that require a specific format, value, or length provide this information as a text description.
	3.3.1	If utilized, form validation errors are presented in an efficient, intuitive, and accessible manner. The error is clearly identified, quick access to the problematic element is provided, and user is allowed to easily fix the error and resubmit the form.

Labels or Instructions	3.3.2	Sufficient labels, cues, and instructions for required interactive elements are provided at the beginning of the form or set of fields via instructions, examples, properly positioned form labels, and/or fieldsets/legends. (Note: Placeholder text should not be used alone to convey label or instruction.)
Error Suggestion	3.3.3	If an input error is detected (via client-side or server-side validation), provide suggestions for fixing the input in a timely and accessible manner.
Error Prevention (Legal, Financial, Data)	3.3.4.	If the user can change or delete legal, financial, or test data, the changes/deletions can be reversed, verified, or confirmed.
4.1 – Compatible Parsing	4.1.1.A	Significant HTML/XHTML validation/parsing errors are avoided. Check at http://validator.w3.org/
Name, Role, Value	4.1.2	For tree and outline components, custom controls, page tabs, progress bars, form controls, elements with sub-menus, etc., ensure the name and role can be programmatically determined; states, properties, and values that can be set by the user can be programmatically set; and notification of changes to these items is available to user agents, including assistive technologies.
	S02	Users have control over platform accessibility features.

Software <u>Interoperability with</u> Assistive Technology	502	There is no interruption between the application and platform accessibility features.
	S02	The content of text objects and text attributes are rendered to the screen and are programmatically determinable. Text objects are also modifiable with the use of assistive technology.
Applications	503	If the application allows the user to customize the font size, color, type or contrast content in the application remains available and respects the settings.
	503	If the application offers an alternative interface, the alternative meets all other respective standards.
	503	If the application contains multimedia, captions controls are provided at the same menu level as volume controls.
	503	If the application contains multimedia, audio description controls are provided at the same menu level as volume controls.
Authoring Tools	504	Where an application is an authoring tool, it provides the necessary functions to create or edit accessible content in the final format.
	504	Where an application is an authoring tool, when content is converted to another format any supported accessibility information is carried to the final format.

	504	Where an application is an authoring tool and a PDF of content can be created, the generated PDF complies with PDF/UA standards.
	504	Where an application is an authoring tool, prompts are provided to ensure accessible content is created.
	504	Where an application is an authoring tool, any available templates within it meet accessibility criteria.

Additional Resources

For more information about accessibility and remediation, check out the official Splash Box website (https://www.splashbox.com/accessibility) and blog (https://www.splashbox.com/blog).

Jenny Hale Woldt

Jenny Woldt is the CEO/Owner of Splash Box Marketing and 615 JJ Entertainment. She is an entrepreneur at heart who built her first business at 13. Her dedication to providing her clients with exceptional service is what led her to develop a 508 Remediation company that has become a front runner in accessibility services. Her passion for the hard of sight developed when her grandfather became completely blind and she recorded herself reading books, so he could continue his nightly bedtime ritual of learning to keep his mind sharp. She is also a wife, a mother of 4, grandmother, occasional podcast guest, travel junkie, photographer, and author. She loves telling stories and kind people have often said, "You should write a book," so she did. Her first work, *The Quiet Place: A Prayer Journal & Walk Through the Holy Land*, is ranked on Amazon's Christian Personal Growth and Christian Inspirational lists and has a five-star average rating. This work is the culmination of her passion for accessibility and 508 remediation, showcasing her expertise. When she's not at work, she can be found traveling and spending time with her family.

Keep in touch with Jenny via the web:
Website: https://www.jennyhalewoldt.com/
Instagram: https://www.instagram.com/jennyhalewoldt/
LinkedIn: https://www.linkedin.com/in/jennywoldt/

Helen Bowen

Helen Bowen, research assistant and editor, is a 508 Remediation Specialist with Splash Box Marketing, where she works to remediate WCAG 2.0-compliant Word, PowerPoint, and PDF documents and forms. Shortly after graduating from Western Carolina University with a degree in Communication, she discovered her love for accessibility and began volunteering to edit and hand-caption weekly services for a local church during the peak of the COVID-19 pandemic. Ever since, she has challenged herself to learn a little more about accessibility every day and recently received her International Association of Accessibility Professionals (IAAP) Certification as a Professional in Accessibility Core Competencies (CPACC).

Keep in touch with Helen via her LinkedIn: https://www.linkedin.com/in/hbowen627

www.ingramcontent.com/pod-product-compliance
Lightning Source LLC
LaVergne TN
LVHW051744050326
832903LV00029B/2704